The Lord Is Our Salvation

Lent

 2015

The Lord Is Our Salvation

KATIE Z. DAWSON

A Lenten Study Based on the Revised Common Lectionary

Abingdon Press / Nashville

THE LORD IS OUR SALVATION
by Katie Z. Dawson

A Lenten Study Based on the Revised Common Lectionary

Copyright © 2014 by Abingdon Press

ISBN-13: 9781426785856

14 15 16 17 18 19 20 21 22 23—10 9 8 7 6 5 4 3 2 1

MANUFACTURED IN THE UNITED STATES OF AMERICA

Contents

Introduction

Sometimes, the clearest way to understand salvation is to look at what is broken, dysfunctional, and messed up in our lives.

The reality of hell looks different in every situation. Sometimes it affects our personal lives through addiction and oppression. Sometimes it affects our communities through injustice or tragedy. Sometimes hell's grasp is subtle, and we deny it's there. But when we become aware of hellish situations, they can help us to see, in contrast, how God comes to bring salvation; we discover the good news Jesus offers in a particular place or to a particular person. Salvation is not a general theory. We claim that Jesus is the Lord of *our* salvation and is doing something to transform *our* lives.

Salvation is "God's deliverance of those in a situation of need . . . resulting in their restoration to wholeness."[1] It is restoration because salvation does not offer something new; it is God's *original* intention for creation. In the beginning, "the earth was without shape or form, it was dark over the deep sea" (Genesis 1:2). God spoke to bring life, light, and truth out of darkness. This intended peace of creation is described by the Hebrew word *shalom.* The word shalom encompasses God's desire that we experience wholeness and well-being, safety and protection, peace and love. God's work of salvation in Jesus Christ rescues us from the hell that has destroyed shalom, so we might live in this peace once more.

We know who God is by what God does. The Scriptures we explore during this season of Lent reveal to us our Lord. Whether it is in the Flood or in Babylon, in the back alleys of Jerusalem or at the ends of the earth, God has acted consistently to bring life out of death, bring light out of darkness, and bring us back into healthy relationship with God and one another. No matter what kind of hell we are facing, the God who created us can redeem us. The cross of Jesus Christ is big enough, wide enough, and powerful enough to save.

However, Christ not only saves us *from* something; he also saves us *for* something. To declare Jesus is the Lord of our salvation is to place our life in God's hands and to accept the covenant of that relationship. It is to trust that Jesus' death, resurrection, and ascension will bring light to the darkest corners of our existence. It is to turn away from the hell that is so familiar to embrace a life of shalom we never thought possible.

Do you have faith that God can do that in your life? Are you ready to accept your salvation?

1. From "Salvation," in *The New Interpreter's Dictionary of the Bible,* Volume 5; page 45.

Keep Me From Drowning

Scriptures for Lent:
The First Sunday
Genesis 9:8-17
1 Peter 3:18-22
Mark 1:9-15

The first time I experienced the power of a flood, I was ten years old. Because my family wasn't personally affected, I was excited about this "once in a lifetime" event. I even had a T-shirt that proclaimed, "I survived the flood!" As we drove through flooded areas, I was awed by the mirrored waters reflecting the sky over fields and roads alike.

Years later, I was a pastor in Marengo, Iowa, along the Iowa River. A levee protected the town, but as rain fell that spring, the waters crept up. Communities surrounding us experienced massive flooding, reaching the tops of bridges, spilling into homes, and bringing life to a standstill. I began to panic. This was not the exciting adventure of my childhood but a horrific experience of loss. Homes and businesses in those nearby communities were gone. Families were stranded. As the waters in my town sat mere inches below the top of the levee, I moved stuff out of the basement, put my cat in my car, and got out of town. All I wanted to do was to be with my husband, and he was helping evacuate a family from a nearby city. My greatest fear was that as bridges closed, I would be stranded on the other side of the river.

It was my first year of ministry, not a full six months into my tenure at this church, and I left its members to fend for themselves. I was young and inexperienced, but looking back, I'm embarrassed by my focus on myself. I was overwhelmed and afraid, and I bailed. Fortunately, the levee held in Marengo that spring. Only basements took in water. For that, I am grateful.

Many things can drown us in life. We can sink in temptation and sin. We can get over our heads in opposition and ridicule as we try to live our faith. We can find ourselves neck deep in the muck and mire of life. So, we cry out for help. But as our readings for this week show, there is someone who hears those cries. And in contrast to my failure as a leader, that someone—our

Lord—does not abandon us. Our Lord stays with us, suffers with us and for us, and prepares our deliverance.

THE RAINBOW
GENESIS 9:8-17

It doesn't take very long before everything goes from "supremely good" (Genesis 1:31) to a big, fat mess. Brothers kill brothers, angels and humans interact inappropriately, and humanity itself is enmeshed in sin and wickedness, immorality and violence. By the time we reach Genesis 6, things are far indeed from the shalom God intended for creation.

As God looks upon creation, only Noah is righteous. God calls him to build a boat. Not just any boat—a ship large enough to hold his family and two of every kind of animal. Shortly after the boat is completed, the skies open up and it begins to rain. The waters sweep every other living thing and person on the earth away. For forty days and forty nights, the rains fall and Noah and those with him on the ark are alone in the world.

God remembers Noah (8:1), and the waters begin to recede. Eventually, the boat settles on dry ground, and Noah and his family come out and give thanks. They had survived, but every living thing that was *not* on Noah's ark is now dead. Earth's population has been wiped out.

We can't comprehend the devastating force of floodwaters unless we go through them ourselves. As Cedar Rapids, Iowa, began to recover from flooding in 2008, I mucked out homes and walked through neighborhoods, praying with folks who'd lost everything. What remained was under inches of mud and silt. The smell was horrendous. Death and mold and decay were everywhere. Blocks of neighborhoods are still boarded up six and seven years later.

When Noah set up his altar and prayed, he was likely surrounded by bloated animals, dead humans, and muck-covered rocks. As the smoke from the offering rose to heaven, God looked at the destruction and made a promise, which can be paraphrased this way:

> Never again will I send a flood to destroy the earth and everything that lives on it. And as a reminder, the rainbow is going to be a sign of that promise, this new covenant. Whenever a storm comes and you see that rainbow, I will remember the promise that I have made to you today.

We may not like this part of the story, where God seems to have a change of mind. God is supposed to be unchanging and not feel regret about the past. But maybe this story isn't about God changing at all. Many other cultures and religions of the time had their own flood stories: gods sending waters to cover the earth. Many of these tales also have a hero who is warned of the flood and who preserves the heritage of his people. It's not surprising that our tradition has a flood story, too. What is surprising, in contrast to those tales, is that the biblical account tells us God is merciful. Our God seeks to save, not destroy.

Ash Wednesday reminds us of our sin, our mortality, and our finite natures. We are all sinners. We are all made of the dust of the earth. We can't save ourselves from drowning in all of that dirt and muck. We might place ourselves in the story and believe we would have been destroyed by the floodwaters.

But our Hebrew ancestors took that familiar story of the flood and retold it with a different ending. Our God made a covenant, a promise, with us. Our God isn't temperamental or callous. Our God seeks relationship and reconciliation. From the very first chapter of Genesis to the very last chapter of Revelation, the message is the same: God loves us, and despite whatever hell we are drowning in, God wants to save us.

This story of destruction and flooding tells us that God made a covenant with all people through Noah. It's the promise of a new relationship in a post-Flood world. Even if "the ideas of the human mind are evil from their youth" (8:21) and we dive headfirst into sin, God will not abandon us or destroy us. God will bring us back to shalom.

In the ancient Near East, the rainbow had been a sign of judgment from the heavens, accompanied by ominous clouds and bolts of lightning shooting forth as arrows to condemn.[1] Yet in this story, as God makes a covenant with all creation, the rainbow itself is transformed. It becomes a symbol of peace and mercy, a symbol of grace even in the midst of judgment.

Rather than gather up wrath and hurl lightning bolts when we do not obey, our Lord sees the rainbow in the sky and looks down upon us without condemnation (9:14-15). Even though we are sinners one and all, God reaches down to us. God, who took a lump of clay and formed us in the divine image, cared for us from the beginning. Our God breathed life itself into us. Our God is merciful and patient.

Though we are drowning in sin, God makes a covenant with Noah to never again cut off all life through floodwaters. In the midst of the death, destruction and loss of the Flood, God blesses Noah's family and calls its members to create life themselves. They are not pristine human beings; they have faults of their own (as the very next verses after this selection remind us), but they now know that every living creature is under the care of the Lord.

God doesn't want to destroy us, even if we are unrighteous and full of sin. God desires not the death of a sinner, but a repentant heart. Our Lord has already set in motion plans to deliver us.

Have you ever felt you needed to be righteous to earn your salvation? How does the promise of the rainbow bring comfort?

A BROKEN CROSS
1 PETER 3:18-22

1752

The Scriptures have the ability both to comfort the afflicted and to afflict the comfortable—at the same time. To those who are overwhelmed by religious oppression, like people in the churches Peter was encouraging or like Christians in parts of the world where others are hostile to Christianity, the message of First Peter offers hope.

While Christians in certain other nations are threatened, most of us in the Western world are not experiencing the hell of persecution. There may be isolated instances where one is forced to deny one's faith under threat, but it is not the norm in our part of the planet.

For a long time, the United States was thought of as a Christian nation, though it never was officially so. Still, there's been a strong Judeo-Christian ethic and language in our politics, government, and culture in general. In a world where the lines between Christ, church, and culture were blurred, faith came easily. Perhaps that was a problem. Too often, the forces of this world gain the upper hand when they cozy up next to faith, and we lose our ability to have a prophetic and truth-filled voice. Rather than a conscientious choice, faith can become a fair-weather habit that props up our politics rather than informs them.

In these last few decades, however, that unity between Christians and the nation has started to unravel. The United States today is one of the biggest mission fields in the world. Many living among us find the church a strange and backward place. Alliances between denominations and political parties are dissolving. We are experiencing not persecution, but neglect. Many people simply do not care about our faith. And sometimes we feel as if we are drowning in a sea of secularism as we try to follow Jesus in this postmodern and post-Christian world.

Our attempts to follow Christ faithfully can even cause conflict within us. This is the natural result of trying to live as citizens of the kingdom of God and practice shalom in the face of very different kinds of kingdoms. How will we respond to that conflict? Are we going to hold our allegiance to Jesus in spite of opposition? Are we willing to sacrifice, even our own lives, in faithfulness to Christ?

In March of 2003, while I was a student at Simpson College in Indianola, Iowa, our country began a war with Iraq. I kept thinking about all of those things I had learned from Jesus, and I felt deep in my bones that this military venture was wrong. In conversations with my roommates and friends, I found others were similarly convinced. Many of us stood together, as Christians, in opposition to the war. If all human beings are children of God, then any life lost is to be mourned. We erected crosses on the lawn in front of the chapel symbolizing the rapidly rising death toll. We intended this as a reminder that there was a real human price to this conflict.

The morning after we placed the crosses, we walked onto campus and found them torn down. Many were broken apart, and the broken pieces were used to spell out "God Bless the USA."

Our campus was torn in two that semester. Faithful people from different Christian perspectives argued with one another. One afternoon, we hung a sheet on the side of our house that read, "Honk if you hate this war." Rocks were thrown through our windows in response. That was a turning point for me. I concluded there was nothing I could say or do to change the minds of those who had already made theirs up. I regretted putting up that sign, which seemed to only escalate the conflict, rather than reach out and speak in love.

In the verses immediately preceding our passage from First Peter, we are encouraged to face opposition with our eyes focused on Jesus: "It is better to suffer for doing good (if this could possibly be God's will) than for doing evil" (3:17). We can endure suffering with faithfulness because Christ suffered on our behalf. He has already been here. Jesus had the worst of this world thrown at him, experienced our death, and was "made alive by the Spirit" (3:18). His resurrection and ascension proclaims that those who stand in the way of salvation, wholeness, and God's shalom will not prevail. The power of the cross as an instrument of oppression is broken. We no longer need to regard it with fear.

Whether we are experiencing active persecution or feeling isolated and neglected, First Peter reminds us that God is still with us. It's a reminder that God has already declared victory over those who have stood or stand today in the way of God's shalom. And the persecuted can be assured that in God's time, victory is theirs, too. William Joseph Dalton says, when persecuted, Christians need to remember the value of suffering for Christ's sake so they can "stand firm and faithful despite their experience of alienation."[2]

Salvation delivers us from enemies only God can conquer. Because we have life in Christ, the one who "rules over all angels, authorities, and powers" (3:22), there is nothing left to fear. As the familiar hymn declares, "This is my Father's world, / O let me ne'er forget that though the wrong seems oft so strong, / God is the ruler yet."[3] In our baptism, we declare our allegiance to the kingdom where God is the ruler. We place our battle in God's hands. Baptism, says 1 Peter 3:21, is "the mark of a good conscience toward God." This does not mean that we are without sin and always choose what is right, but baptism does mark our intended orientation toward God and a desire to live in the way of Jesus.

The season of Lent reminds us that Jesus became one of us and took our life into his own. As he faced the hell of persecution, Jesus did not once curse his enemies. Not once did he wish them harm. Not once did he become like them. He shows us how to love, how to forgive, yet also how not to be a passive bystander in the process.

John Mabry describes nonviolent resister Nelson Mandela as "an imitator of Christ, not because he suffered in prison, but because he held out for peace and justice, and led a nation to resurrection."[4] God has reached out to us through the resurrection of Jesus Christ, and if we choose to be followers of Jesus, the power of resurrection spills over into everything we do.

I needed that spirit as we engaged in difficult conversations on campus that spring. I needed to stand firm in my faith and continue to call for peace, but I needed to do so in a way that was faithful to the life of Jesus Christ. Yelling at one another and speaking past each other did not lead to transformation. Only prayer, compassion, and the willingness to build relationships can bring about shalom for ourselves and others.

When did you feel a conflict between your faith and other allegiances? What gave you strength in that situation?

NOW IS THE TIME!
MARK 1:9-15

1435

"Now is the time! Here comes God's kingdom! Change your hearts and lives, and trust this good news!" (1:15).

To repent, to change our hearts and lives, means to turn around and move in the opposite direction. God's covenant with Noah reminds us of God's steadfast love and mercy, but it doesn't restore us to God's shalom. We are still drowning in sin, still craving a fresh start, still crying out for deliverance. "Now is the time!" Jesus declares.

There's a parable about a man stranded by a flood. He crawls on the roof and prays for God to rescue him. A firefighter comes by in a boat, but the man refuses the would-be rescuer and continues to pray. A police officer comes by on a jet ski, but the man refuses help. The floodwaters rise and overwhelm him, and he dies. As he stands by Peter at the pearly gates, he cries out in frustration, "Why didn't God answer my prayers?" Peter responds, "We sent two boats!"

When we pray for rescue, we don't always know whom to trust. Who is this Jesus? How do we know he's from God? Why should we trust him? In a world that overwhelms us with false claims and promises, we can't simply drop everything for some "nobody" from Galilee. So Mark begins his Gospel by making clear that Jesus Christ *is* the one we have been waiting for. God has patiently loved us and laid the foundation for the good news of salvation. The moment has finally arrived.

John the Baptist sets the stage by calling people to a life of repentance and confession of sin. Jesus goes to John, enters the water, symbolically walking alongside us in our life of sin. He dives into the murky waters of our lives, transforming a simple ritual into a sacred promise. As Jesus rises up out of the water, the voice of God speaks, "You are my Son, whom I dearly love; in you I find happiness" (1:11).

The Messiah, the Son of God, was the one foretold in the Scriptures. The Son of God would bring about God's salvation. This moment of his baptism, like no other, confirms for us who this person was and is and what he does. God creates us, claims us, names us, and saves us. Through Jesus Christ, we become the sons and daughters of God. Through the waters of baptism, we, too, hear the voice calling out: *In you, I find happiness. You are mine.*

But salvation doesn't stop at baptism. Our declaration of faith is not the end of this journey. No, as soon as Jesus hears that voice, the Spirit of God whisks him away into the wilderness. There, for forty days and nights, he is tempted. The wild beasts surround him, and angels take care of him. Jesus didn't pack an emergency kit. He didn't give excuses for why he couldn't go. He went and completely and utterly put his life in the Father's hands. We might compare these forty days to the forty years of Moses and the Israelites in the wilderness. With the presence of those wild beasts and angels, our minds might wander to the Garden of Eden. We are reminded of people who were called to be God's people and depend upon God's grace and deliverance, but who failed to fully trust in their Lord.

Mark's account of the wilderness is not a long tale of temptations and failures and fits and starts of faith, but a few words about faithfulness: Jesus was tempted by Satan. He was among the animals. The angels took care of him. No drama. No fuss. No mistakes. No surrender to sin. In this story, we discover what it means to remain faithful to God. Jesus fully depends upon the Father, the animals are peaceful, the angels provide, and Satan—well he disappears. This wilderness is shalom. As commentator Pheme Perkins says, "Jesus had already broken Satan's power before his ministry began."[5]

We, too, are invited to depend on God's salvation, to place our lives, our time, our energy, and our resources in God's hands. The Lenten wilderness invites us to let go of our barriers and resistance. We can relinquish control, because we trust in our Lord to provide. Trust is important, you see, for we cannot let go if we do not believe that God loves us. Our very faith depends upon the actions of a God who loves and forgives and offers salvation. Because God freely offers grace, because God's hand of salvation reaches to us as we cry for rescue, we can grab hold firmly and not let go. "Now is the time!"

My grandparents had dimmer switches on the lamps in their living room. When I was a child, they seemed magical; as a grownup, I Googled how they work. The source of electricity in a dimmer switch never changes. It is always flowing at one hundred percent, much like the power of God's love, grace, and mercy offered through Jesus Christ. But in the mechanism is a resistor, designed to conduct electricity poorly. As the knob is turned, the resistance is increased or decreased, and the output of the power changes. When the resistor is fully on, most of the initial energy is lost, the voltage drops, and the light is weak and dim. But when the resistor is barely on, very little of the electrical charge is lost as it travels through the circuit, and it illuminates the light bulb to its full strength.

Even though Jesus enters the hell of our lives and invites us to turn our lives fully toward him, sometimes we only turn around a little bit. We put up resistance. We make excuses. We want to stay where we are. Perhaps we think living our faith costs too much. The amount of resistance we put up varies on different days and in different seasons. Some days we are open to God's love and power. Other times, we erect every roadblock we can think of: "I'm too old;" "I'm too tired;" "I'm too poor."

No matter how much resistance we put up, the power of God is still flowing at one hundred percent. In God's salvation, we have everything we need for shalom. Jesus is ready to open the kingdom to us. He went to the cross to bring us salvation. When we truly repent, when we truly turn our lives around 180 degrees and place our whole selves into God's hands, we throw the resistor out. In the waters of baptism, we die to our old selves and are made alive by the Spirit. And with that power, God gives us what we need to keep from returning to our old lives.

Are you drowning in sin and chaos? Well, now is the time! Here comes God's kingdom! Change your hearts and lives, and trust this good news!

Where are you resisting God's grace in your life? What needs to happen for you to trust in the good news?

1. From *The New Interpreter's Bible*, Volume I (Abingdon Press, 1994); page 400.

2. From *The New Interpreter's Bible*, Volume XII, cited by David L. Bartlett (Abingdon Press, 1998); page 294.

3. From "This is My Father's World," Lyrics by Maltbie D. Babcock, *The United Methodist Hymnal* (Copyright © 1989 by The United Methodist Publishing House); 144.

4. From *Crisis & Communion: The Remythologization of the Eucharist—Past, Present, and Future,* by John R. Mabry (Apocryphile Press, 2005); page 129.

5. *The New Interpreter's Bible*, Volume VIII (Abingdon Press, 1995); page 536.

Trust and Obey

Scriptures for Lent:
The Second Sunday
Genesis 17:1-7, 15-16
Romans 4:13-25
Mark 8:31-38

A few years ago, my in-laws talked me into whitewater rafting on the Menominee River. At that time of year, there were class-3 rapids, which our guide informed us were, "dangerous enough to have fun." In the caravan of three rafts and twenty riders, I was in the first group and the front row. It was exhilarating.

Whitewater rafting requires trust. As a rider, you trust the guide with your safety. As a guide, you trust the riders to listen and obey your directions. That trust becomes a pact, a covenant, and both parties must uphold their side. This week, we explore God's covenant with Abraham and its fulfillment in Jesus Christ. As God lays out the divine plan (land, descendants, making Abraham the father of nations), Abraham has to trust that God can do these things. He has to believe God can bring life out of death, a nation out of a barren womb, something major out of something meager.

We have to trust as well. We have to believe in God's power to resurrect. We have to have faith in God's power to make us righteous. We have to hold fast to the promise, even through times of difficulty. It's like coming to the top of a drop on the rapids. You can see the danger that lies ahead, but you can't go back. So you either panic and cower in fright, or you trust the instructions of the guide and dig in with your paddles and row with all your might. No matter how scary it gets, no matter how impossible it seems, you know the guide has been on these waters before. You trust the guide knows the way through the rocks. You believe that even if you make a mistake and fall out of the boat, the guide will get you back in.

In life, our guide is the Lord. If we take that first step and trust, God will be there. He will lead us in his paths. God will help us carry the crosses we have to bear. God will make sure that we get through this rocky and sometimes even hellacious ride to the smooth water on the other side.

LORDS AND CONTRACTS
GENESIS 17:1-7, 15-16

Abram was at the ripe old age of ninety-nine when God's great invitation came: "Walk with me and be trustworthy. I will make a covenant between us and I will give you many, many descendants" (17:1b-2). Covenants are central to our life of faith. Last week, we explored the covenant between God and Noah and all of creation after the Flood. This week, the covenant between the Lord and Abram (Abraham) lays the foundation for the salvation God intends for the world.

In the time of Abram, many lords and kings ruled over city-states and territories. We get a glimpse of these rulers as Abram settles in the land of Canaan and navigates tricky political terrain. The rulers and their peoples often had covenantal relationships. One such covenant was a "suzerain-vassal" treaty. In this type of covenant, the suzerain (ruler or lord) set the terms of the relationship and told the vassals (people) what they must do. Whether the king gained power through acclaim, violence, money, or conniving, such a contract shored up support and income. For the people, the covenant brought order to chaos and promised at least temporary peace and protection.

In popular culture, lords are everywhere. You can find Lord Grantham on the BBC series *Downton Abbey* and the Lords Stark and Lannister in the show *Game of Thrones*. While these are decidedly different genres and appeal to different audiences, they each draw on a similar concept of a protector whose duty it is to watch over those in their lands. *Downton Abbey* is set in early twentieth-century England, where Lord Grantham oversees an estate and the people of the village who depend upon him for their well-being and employment. The people, in turn, are contractually bound to the welfare of their lord. In a fictional world with hints of medieval times, the lords of *Game of Thrones* uphold justice and provide protection for those under their domain. In return, the lesser lords swear loyalty to the house they serve and fight to protect its honor. It's clear the relationship between a lord and his people could be benevolent or hostile.

A suzerain-vassal treaty is a contract between radically unequal partners, be they medieval lords and peasants or an estate owner and tenant farmers. This is a promise in which one party has most of the power to dictate the conditions; the other can but give their obedience, trust, and loyalty. This is a common understanding of salvation as well: protection, safety, preservation of a way of life. It is the assurance that someone stronger than you has your back. And you will do whatever it takes to be faithful, to ensure you remain under that lord's protection.

Since any covenant in which God is a partner is by its very nature one between radically unequal partners, we might want to call such covenants suzerain-vassal contracts as well. What is very different about the covenant between God and Abram, however, is that this is not simply an agreement between a ruler and a group of the ruler's contemporaries. The covenant with Abram lays out God's intentions, not just for the life of Abram and Sarai, but for the salvation of generations. This is an "enduring covenant" (17:7) that will reach far into the future and encompass all of creation. Still, like a king rallying his subjects to battle, God reaches out to Abram and calls him to be faithful, to trust, and to embark on a grand adventure.

To embark on a great adventure, to take a step of faith on a dare or challenge, can change your life. In the 2012 film, *The Hobbit*, Bilbo asks the wizard Gandalf, "Can you promise me that I will come back?" To which the wizard replies, "No. And if you do . . . you will not be the same." It reminds me of an experience I had at Christmas one year, when I was looking through photos of a cruise my grandparents had taken. I viewed the obligatory shots of landscapes visited, but then I discovered a photo of my grandmother bungee-jumping. At sixty-five years old, she had stood on the edge of a bridge and leaped. It completely changed the way I saw her.

When God first initiates the covenant with Abram, God says, "Leave your land, your family . . . for the land that I will show you. I will make of you a great nation and will bless you" (Genesis 12:1-2). Of course, the promise that a great nation would come from him meant that though Abram was childless at this point, he would eventually have a child so that his line could continue. At seventy-five, he picked up everything and went. He began a journey that day, heading out for something brand new. At seventy-five!

After ten years and many adventures, Abram is wealthy and successful by the world's standards, but still childless. In that culture, the lack of descendants meant that when a man died, all that he had lived for was lost. But again, God promises land and blessing and descendants (15:1-21). Here's where it gets even more interesting: This story isn't only about Abram; Sarai, his wife, is along for the journey, too. Knowing she's barren and too old to conceive, she proposes a solution. She wants to be faithful to God and give her husband children, so she gives her servant to Abram as a wife (16:1-4). But to make a long story short: Ishmael is born, Sarai is angry, Hagar is mistreated, and no one is happy.

After thirteen years go by, God speaks, renewing the covenant once again: "Walk with me and be trustworthy. I will make a covenant between us and I will give you many, many descendants" (17:1b-2). At ninety-nine years old, some of us would find the invitation simply to walk to be difficult! But God also urges Abram to be utterly trustworthy and faithful in everything. Note, it doesn't say "perfect," even if some translations use the word "blameless." God wants Abram to be loyal and faithful and to trust with all of his heart. If Abram can do that, then there is more to this adventure. God will make Abram the ancestor of nations, completely transforming his life.

As a reminder that in this covenant everything changes, God renames Abram; he's now Abraham (from "exalted father" to "father of a multitude"). This covenant is also for Abram's wife Sarai. God has not forgotten her and declares that she has a role to play in this unbelievable promise. God renames her Sarah, saying, "I will bless her so that she will become nations" (17:16). It doesn't matter that she is well past childbearing age. It doesn't matter that Abraham and Sarah are old and worn out. God asks them to trust, to take the leap of faith, and to bring life into this world.

God invites them to believe in the impossible. God invites them to believe there can be life in barren places. God invites them to trust.

What does it mean for God to be the Lord of your salvation? Where has the Lord protected and guided you?

DISCOVERING OUR ANCESTORS
ROMANS 4:13-25

The women in my family make an annual pilgrimage to south central Iowa for genealogical reasons. Aunts, cousins, sisters, and daughters cram into a van and drive through the hilly countryside and down old dirt roads, looking for our ancestors. Along the way, we have many adventures. Driving the poorly maintained road to one forgotten cemetery requires guts and determination after the spring thaw and fresh rain. More than once, we nearly get stuck in the mud and are in danger of sliding into a ravine. We carry with us the wisdom and folly of old wives' tales, always making sure when we pee on the side of the road that we spit in it—lest we "get a sty in your eye!"

We stop for meals in little diners and buy baskets from an Amish family. But the true aim of our trips is to live into a legacy. As we seek the cemeteries where generations of Pickens and Liles and Hazen and Cox families are buried, we are securing records for future generations. We are gathering stories of my grandfather and great aunts' generations so they do not fade into dust. We discover old family dynamics, never talked about, that shed light on current relationships. In a forgotten, old cemetery, we tend an overgrown patch of irises and take some to plant in our own gardens. The lives of our ancestors are taking root in our future.

When the apostle Paul looks back to the faith of Abraham and God's covenant with that patriarch, Paul is not merely pointing out an example; he's inviting us to claim the father of nations as *our* ancestor (Romans 4:13-16, especially 16)— not by blood, religious tradition, or law, but by faith. In Romans, Paul writes to a community of Christians, both Gentile and Jewish, who can't figure out how to get along.[1] Trying to piece together a family of stepsisters and half-brothers and the strange kid down the street, Paul points to the things they, and we, have in common. He is inviting all of these new Christians to make the faith of Abraham their own. If we have that same faith, we are part of the same family.

But what was this faith of Abraham? What was the amazing thing he believed that was "credited to him as righteousness" (4:22), which Paul urged Christians to believe as well? Abraham lived before Moses held the Ten Commandments in his hands and before Mary gave birth to Jesus Christ, so what could his faith possibly have to do with what the early Christians believed and what we are called to believe here and now?

We need to look at Paul's understanding of righteousness. He gets the term from the temple courts of his day; it can be used both to describe the winner in a legal case and the judge who oversees the verdict. The judge is obligated to be righteous or just, to hear the case fairly and impartially, seeking to defend those who are vulnerable. The righteous person in the court is the one who wins the case, the one proven to have been trustworthy and true. Either by finding them innocent or by declaring their claims correct, the judge pronounces them righteous or vindicated. Theirs is the justice. They are the ones who can shout to the world, "HA! I was right."

Let's translate that concept to our faith. God is righteous like the trustworthy judge. God seeks justice for the vulnerable and remains faithful to the covenant. That covenant provides ground not to give us what we deserve, but to bring everything back into right relationship, to restore us to God's shalom. God, in his love, mercy, and compassion, sent Jesus into the world to stand by us in the courtroom of life. Our faith makes us righteous when what we believe and trust in our lives is actually true. Paul says it simply: Abraham had faith in "the God who gives life to the dead and calls things that don't exist into existence" (4:17).

As we saw in Genesis, this was not an easy thing to believe. Abraham and Sarah often wavered in their own trust of that promise. They laughed at the possibility. They tried to do it their own way. But in the end, it was their faith that brought life into their midst as they finally and fully embraced God's plan. No matter how many bumps in the road they hit before they got to the final destination, they still got there. They made it, in spite of their own self-inflicted mud traps and ravine detours. Abraham believed God could take his ninety-nine-year-old body and Sarah's empty womb and create life . . . and God did. Paul can look back upon their lives and say that Abraham "grew strong in faith and gave glory to God. He was fully convinced that God was able to do what he promised" (4:20-21). Abraham trusted, and he was right.

The singular question of faith for every Christian is not any different from Abraham's. Do we believe, in spite of every scientific or philosophical reality, as impossible as it might be, that God "gives life to the dead and calls things that don't exist into existence?" That is, after all, what the gospel is all about. Do we "have faith in the one who raised Jesus our Lord from the dead" (4:24)?

Our belief that God has raised Jesus from the dead and can forgive our sins is not some pie-in-the-sky fantasy or a story we have told to make ourselves feel better. We are right! The resurrection of Jesus Christ is his vindication. It is proof that life can come out of death. And with it comes the final verdict that light conquers darkness, sin is wiped away, and hell is replaced with God's shalom. Just as Jesus took on our mistakes, out of sheer love and grace, he gives back to us his righteousness. This is the covenant that God has made with everyone who trusts that the Lord can bring life out of death: Jesus will stand by our side, forgive our sins, and we, too, will be credited as righteous.

Abraham's faith is not about some magic words or formula; it is about trusting with his whole being that the God who created this world out of nothing and brings life from what is dead can therefore justify the sinner. If you and I can trust like that, if we are willing to faithfully and wholeheartedly love and serve the God who raised Jesus from the dead, then we are part of the family of Abraham. We are part of Paul's family. We are part of a family of imperfect people who have nevertheless been saved by God's grace. Our faith has been credited to us as righteousness.

Think of a time you were convinced you were right, in spite of opposition. Do you have that same feeling in your spiritual life?

CROSSES AND ELECTRIC CHAIRS
MARK 8:31-38

Our wholehearted trust in the God who can bring life out of death sometimes wavers when it's actually put to the test. Even the most faithful and willing, like Peter, can struggle with trusting and following Jesus.

As one of the disciples, Peter thought he was fully behind Jesus. Thus, when Jesus and his band stopped just outside of Caesarea Philippi to refocus their mission, Peter was ready. "Who do you say that I am?" asked Jesus. "You are the Christ," Peter declared (8:29). But Peter didn't understand the depths of what he'd uttered. He spoke words that were full of power and justice and victory, but Jesus had a much different path in mind. "The Human One must suffer . . . and be killed, and then . . . rise from the dead," Jesus said (8:31). The path to victory goes through defeat. The journey toward life passes through death. To receive forgiveness, we have to take a long, difficult look at our sinful lives.

The word *must* occurs twice in this passage from Mark, once in verse 31 and once in verse 34. That tells us a lot about God's plan. The Human One *must* undergo great suffering. If you want to follow Christ and place your faith in God, then you *must* say no to yourself and take up your cross. This is the only way. Jesus calls us to

- come after him and follow him;
- do what is necessary, not what is easy;
- let go of all the stuff we think we need and relationships that hinder our discipleship;
- trust that God's way is better, because in the end it is the only way that leads to life;
- take up our cross.

Today, we wear beautiful crosses around our necks and on our lapels. We put them in our churches. But we sometimes transform the challenging call of the cross into a romantic idea of the burdens we bear. I've heard many people talk about illnesses or a difficult family member or a financial hardship they are experiencing as "a cross to bear." Too often, we have turned our problems into a semi-spiritual truth and therefore refuse to address them.

Actually, Jesus' invitation to take up the cross could be translated today as, "Put yourself in the electric chair." In Jesus' world, the cross was an instrument of capital punishment for criminals and traitors of the Roman Empire. Our cross is not an illness, difficult people, or financial hardships; it's the conflict that arises because of following Christ, the result of things we do in Jesus' name. When Jesus challenges us to take up our cross, he's asking us to take on the reality of hell and embrace the consequences of following him.

I attended a community forum on suicide and depression among middle- and high-school students. One teacher talked about a student named Jennifer, who was ridiculed by her peers because she goes to a church youth group. In a culture where belonging is everything, this truly was a cross for Jennifer to bear. In a broadcast about life at Harper High School in Chicago, a young man named Deonte tells about trying to avoid gang life and cling to his Christian identity. To follow Christ in his community means that he can't go outside or around his neighborhood. To avoid the gangs, he has been homebound (aside from school) for three years. "At times I feel lonely. At times, I would want to have some friends. Because I'm not really friends with anybody." [2] His is a cross to bear.

Most of us will not face violence because we have been attending church. We won't be arrested like Paul for speaking openly of our faith. We won't be dragged in front of a firing squad simply for being a follower of Christ. But that doesn't mean that we can sit back and relax. In fact, I think this passage of Scripture is an imperative *to seek out* our cross, to live our lives and to share the gospel with the world in a way that draws attention. We are called to go to places of hell and stand with people like Jennifer or Deonte and help them to carry the crosses they bear. We can refuse to send our children to Sunday sporting events. We can speak out against national and world issues that harm life rather than restore it.

I appreciate that my church has a whole book full of our stances on issues like the death penalty, war, torture, and the environment. They are all positions that as a church we feel best express the shalom God intends and how God has called us to live with one another. We take up our cross and work for that shalom by writing letters to congressional leaders, attending protests, boycotting goods, even getting arrested during acts of civil disobedience. All of these things are forms that discipleship may take as we follow Christ and proclaim shalom. There may be crosses we have to bear as a result. We might draw out the ire of a colleague. We might be fired from our job. We might even be arrested. But remember the call. It's easy to stay on the paths we are on, to take the safe road, but if we want to truly save our lives, we must trust our Lord, we must dive in headfirst into the life of Christ; we *must* take up our crosses.

At the cross, several things fight with one another: life and death, hope and despair, shalom and hell. And Jesus Christ takes these struggling forces through the cross and comes out on the other side victoriously. In the end there is only life; there is only hope; there is only God. And when the Human One, "comes in the Father's glory with the holy angels" (8:38), the faithful will be by his side. If we trust in the God who created us out of nothing and can raise the dead, then we can endure any suffering or rejection. We know, we believe, we trust that we have already been delivered from hell.

Where is Jesus asking you to step out in faith? Who might get upset in the process?

1. From *The New Interpreter's Bible*, Volume X (Abingdon, 2002); page 406.
2. From "Harper High School, Part One." Aired 02.15.2013. Copyright © Chicago Public Media & Ira Glass.

Truth and Carnival Mirrors

Scriptures for Lent:
The Third Sunday
Exodus 20:1-17
1 Corinthians 1:18-25
John 2:13-22

From the beginning of time, God has been working to bring shalom into the world. We can glimpse the outline of that shalom in the laws of Scripture, which Bible scholar Walter Brueggemann describes as "God's full intention for the life of creation."[1] So quickly, however, is that intention distorted in our lives.

My extended family was vacationing in northwest Iowa and visited a lovely little amusement park on the shore of Lake Okoboji. In the park, we climbed through a tilted house. Walking sideways on crooked steps as the ceilings seem to shrink above you feels odd and disconcerting. We know what a house should look like and feel like, and this was most certainly not it. From there, my niece grabbed my hand and dragged me to the house of mirrors. As we stood in front of skinny mirrors and fat mirrors and wavy mirrors, she giggled and pointed as we were transformed into creatures we didn't recognize. I had mile-long legs one minute and a neck as long as a giraffe's the next. We laughed and told stories about what it would be like to live with really tall tummies and itty-bitty heads.

Children enjoy such mirrors, but we adults may find them less amusing. We are self-conscious about our bodies. The distortion brings our flaws into greater focus, takes what we prefer to hide and blows it out of proportion, or reduces our best features to something grotesque. Often, even our everyday mirrors don't flatter us and we see the parts of ourselves we find undesirable: the single gray hair in a beard; the crow's-feet around our eyes; the profile of our nose.

Life can sometimes be like looking in funhouse mirrors of our own making, where we start to believe what we see is reality. But in the Scriptures we explore for this week, we see how God turns upside down the world as we know it to show us a more excellent way. Whether in the thundering voice of Mount Sinai, the foolishness of the cross, or God's presence among us, our crooked walls come tumbling down and the distortions of our mirrors fall away.

"WON'T YOU BE MY NEIGHBOR?"[2]
EXODUS 20:1-17

Mr. Rogers welcomed me into his home many afternoons as I was growing up. Although it was "only" a television program, he created a world where children were loved, valued, and taught what it meant to be a neighbor. It was so simple and yet such a stark contrast to other messages that bombarded me as a child: fighting mutant turtles and power rangers, the pressure to succeed, and all of the stuff you were supposed to buy as a with-it girl in the 1980's.

It was only much later in life that I learned that Rev. Fred Rogers was a pastor and an educator. His ministry exemplified what it means to love God and to love your neighbor with your entire life. He once said, "I've always tried to love my neighbor as myself . . . delighting every day in the lavish gifts of God, whom I've come to believe is the greatest appreciator of all."[3] That intimate connection between our love of neighbor and love of God is behind the commandments God speaks on Mount Sinai. They are the two rules that form the community of God's shalom. Like a blueprint, they show us God's plans for creation.

God comes not to individuals who have been living perfect lives, but to a group of liberated slaves who had known nothing but oppression, injustice, and the distortion of God's will for humanity. As God frees them, they flee through the desert and witness unbelievable miracles. They travel for three months and battle hunger, thirst, and human enemies along the way. By the end of their journey they are tired, sore, and grumpy. But finally, they arrive at the base of a mountain so they can meet their Lord.

With thunder and earthquakes, lighting and noise, God speaks. Like the voice calling out in the chaos of the earth "without shape or form" (Genesis 1:1), God speaks, but this time, what is created is not the world, but a people. God makes a self-introduction as their liberator and lays out what it means for them to respond to their salvation: Love me, love one another.

The Israelites had been in a crooked house for far too long. Systems of abuse, manipulation, and scarcity had been bred into their bones during their long years of slavery. Yet their cries for deliverance were the sign that they knew something was not right about the slanted floors and claustrophobic walls of Egypt. God's message to them was simple: Give me your faithfulness and allegiance, and the distorted hell of your past will become a distant memory. This is the blueprint for the household of God; this is the plan for God's shalom. At the heart of this blueprint are the Ten Commandments.

The first three commandments tell us who this architect is: a jealous God, a powerful God, ever present and active in our lives, yet utterly beyond our reach. These commandments make clear that nothing on heaven or earth can ever compare to the Lord: not idols, not kings, not even other gods. If we try to tame or reduce God or use God for our own ends, we will be the ones who suffer. But if we love and serve God, we will continue in the divine and gracious love. God desires a relationship with these slaves and servants and "nobodies."

The rest of the commandments establish the new social norms for the people of God. They help to erase one of the greatest lies of all: that a human life is but a cog in a machine, a deception that the living hell of abuse in the land of Egypt had been pounding into the Israelites. Cogs in machines do not get tired or need anything, and they can easily be replaced. Cogs have no feelings or hopes or dreams. In the distorted reality of this world, we find ourselves trapped in economic systems and a frenzy of work and consumption. Sitting in a cubicle or standing on an assembly line, we are perhaps not too far away from the mortar and bricks and hard labor of Egypt (Exodus 1:14). We cry out to be heard and seen, and we seek those things that will set us apart and help us to feel less like a machine and more like a person. In doing so, we may trample on the person next to us.

This is not the shalom God intended, but the remaining commandments help us to be restored to its promises. As we roll out the blueprint, we glimpse the peace and joy we can find by following them: Sabbath is a great equalizer where we can take a deep breath and celebrate God's goodness and one another. Family helps us to remember, in order to hang onto the promises of the covenant. Every life is sacred and precious. Period. No one is replaceable. Every individual is valued and offered an opportunity for redemption and a place in the community. Marriage provides not only security but also opportunity for growth and fulfillment of our yearning for connection. Our relationships become ones "of mutuality that are genuinely life-giving, nurturing, enhancing, and respectful," as Walter Brueggemann says.[4] Commands about property give us the opportunity to think not only about the personal belongings of others but also about what each of us truly needs to sustain our lives. In God's shalom, what we give to the poor is only what already rightfully belongs to God. We focus on how we can help create the conditions of life for others, weighing their needs against our desires. A life of honesty creates space for telling the truth about injustice in community and the knowledge that we will be listened to and valued and respected for who we are and what we say. And finally, in desiring God above all else, we discover that we truly have been blessed with abundance. Our lives are filled with gratitude as we share from what we have been given and celebrate with our neighbors their own blessings.

As we stray from God's intentions for this creation, we continue to live in a crooked house that is claustrophobically confining and sloped toward injustice. The Ten Commandments show us God's foundation for our life in relationship to our Lord and to one another.

Where is your neighborhood, country, or world sloped toward injustice? What would happen if we truly put God first and really loved our neighbors as ourselves?

THE WISDOM OF FOOLS
1 CORINTHIANS 1:18-25

My mother told me I couldn't get married until I finished college. While she was a student, working on a business degree in her early twenties, she met my father, fell in love, and dropped out of school for work and a family. She wanted to see us succeed where she had not, and so she instilled in my brothers and me that our educations took priority. In my case, that meant my husband and I dated for seven-and-a-half years. At that point, I had not only finished my bachelor's degree, but I was in the home stretch of my Master of Divinity.

Underlying my mom's advice was a belief that educational attainment determines our future and status in the world. Guidance counselors and teachers echoed that refrain, so my friends and I pushed one another to succeed. And it was something that my mom, herself, continued to seek. In December of 2006, she graduated with her bachelor's degree from the same institution she had entered in the fall of 1977.

An education is one of the vehicles for attaining the "American Dream." Forty-three percent of people who were born into the bottom rung of the economic ladder remain there as adults. But a college degree makes you five times as likely to experience upward mobility.[5] Analysis from the 2010 Census indicates that the earning difference between a bachelor's degree and a high school diploma is roughly $550,000 over the lifetime of an individual.[6]

We who have higher education degrees can sign our official documents with a string of letters indicating our educational attainment. It's a source of status and power for our society, as it was in Corinth during Paul's time. In this cosmopolitan city of the educated and powerful, the Christian faith began to have influence. Yet the status and power derived from wisdom in the city seeped into the community of faith and caused conflict. The sages and rhetoricians who were given a platform in the church gave fancy speeches, but often forgot the core of the gospel in what they said. Paul implies this in the verse immediately preceding our reading: "Christ didn't send me to preach the good news with clever words so that Christ's cross won't be emptied of its meaning" (1:17). In the process, the voices of the less powerful were drowned out. It would be as if Dr. Somebody stood up at the church council meeting and would not allow anyone else to speak because she had a doctorate. Or if another individual felt like he could not add anything to the conversation because he had dropped out of high school.

Paul uses different criteria for what it means to be a Christian. "The message of the cross is foolishness to those who are being destroyed. But it is the power of God for those of us who are being saved" (1:18). He's telling them that everyone who belongs to the community of Jesus is being saved. *This* defines who they are, not whether they are Jews or Greeks or wise or unlearned (1:24).

In the community of faith, the wisdom of the world, when faced with the wisdom of God, does not have power. This is not to say that wisdom and education have no place in the Christian faith. But if we cling to knowledge as what defines our identity, we will miss the point of the gospel. As Christians today, one of our greatest failings is letting the values of this world define the life of our church. Without realizing it, without intending to, we allow "wisdom" to separate us. We self-segregate with congregations of the wealthy and educated worshipping on a different side of town from churches made up of the poor with GEDs. Connections between the two might be made out of a charitable spirit, but ministry of the "wise" happens *to* those "less well off" rather than *with* them.

We put the bankers on the finance committee and construction workers on the trustees committee, and we ask the teachers to run the Sunday school program. That may be appropriate in terms of placing people where their spiritual gifts can be used, but we sometimes don't allow for the unique and amazing ways the Holy Spirit equips unexpected people for extraordinary ministry.

Yet, says Paul, it is not through the world's wisdom that we come to know God, but through the "foolishness of preaching" the gospel (1:21). We know our Lord through the story of the life, death, and resurrection of Jesus. His cross defines our relationships with one another and with our Lord. And the wisdom of the cross and the power of God are available to all, no matter how many degrees we have or haven't earned or where our monthly checks come from.

The wisdom and power of this world is no match for Christ, who is God's true wisdom and God's true power. What we declare in the cross of Jesus Christ might appear to the world a message of humiliation and shame, "a scandal to Jews and foolishness to Gentiles" (verse 23). But when we cling to that cross with faith, when we put our full trust in the Lord, we begin to define true wisdom and true value. We find the strength and hope we need to receive true shalom.

When we cling instead to the values of the world, the cross becomes a stumbling block for not only our faith, but for others as well. Seeking our identity in the wisdom of *this* world will find us falling back into the hell of a dog-eat-dog landscape. Like the carnival mirrors in the funhouse, the wisdom of the world can give us a distorted view that we are good enough, that we have enough of the answers, and that we fully understand God. Like a mirror that makes us look puffed up and filled out, we start to believe we are more important and more knowledgeable than we really are. We begin to believe that salvation comes because of having the right opinions or titles or by the crosses we wear and the music we listen to.

On the flip side, there are mirrors that make us look smaller than we really are, that shrink our heads and whittle our bodies down and make us appear as shrunken beings. We believe if we can't think of beautiful words for a prayer, we can't pray at all. We start to feel as if our lack of worldly possessions reflects a poor spiritual life as well.

Yet when we look to the cross, our carnival-mirror distortions resolve. We discover that the Lord who brings life out of death has turned this world as we know it upside down. And God has not called some distorted image; no, God has called *us*. We are rich and poor, wise and foolish, doctors and dropouts. And God promises to give us the only wisdom and power that truly matter.

What has typically defined your identity in your church community? Where might you serve in the church if your primary identity is as a disciple of Jesus?

TURNING TABLES
JOHN 2:13-22

There are times we think of Jesus as a nice and simple guy, a gentle soul, a friend to walk beside us and listen to our thoughts. But in reality, Jesus turns our world upside down and inside out. He does the unexpected, shows up in unexpected places, loves the unlovable, calls the unworthy, and brings us life through his death. Instead of allowing us to stay comfortably where we are, the Jesus we encounter in the Scriptures challenges life and faith as we know it.

In this passage from John, Jesus goes to Jerusalem to take part in Passover. It is an annual festival, celebrating the story of the exodus from Egypt. As part of this festival, thousands of people would have come to Jerusalem for the eight-day celebration. Those making a long trip would not have brought with them the animals required for sacrifices, but the streets and the Temple itself would have been packed with vendors offering the animals for sale. Others exchanged currency so that tithes and offerings could be been made in coinage that did not bear a human image (the emperor), as Greek and Roman coins did.

This was the normal, expected way of doing things. Sure, there might have been some who took advantage of pilgrims, but for the most part, this was routine life in the Temple, especially around the holy days. Without these vendors, the system simply did not work. And this structure, with its rules and order, vendors and priests, were all a part of what any individual had to navigate to come into the presence of God. You jumped through the hoops because that was the system, the arrangement that existed. But as God reaches out to save us, to restore us, to redeem us, some systems need to change. Our God decides to become one of us; to lay aside glory and be born among us. In the end, God took up residence not within the curtains of the inner sanctuary in that Temple, but in the life of Jesus of Nazareth. And so for John, this is the moment in the Scriptures when a new understanding of the Temple is born. For John, this is the moment when the old and the new dwelling places of the Lord collide.

Jesus not only overturns the tables but also interrupts the entire Temple system. The cattle go one direction; the people go another. Coins are lying everywhere, cages are overturned, and birds are flying past people's faces. There are angry merchants, upset priests, leaders just trying to keep the peace, rattled pilgrims who have traveled for weeks to be here for this one moment. It is absolute chaos. It will take days for the Temple to get up and be fully running again and Passover has practically arrived. All faces turn to Jesus. The religious leaders ask him, "By what authority are you doing these things? What miraculous sign will you show us?" (2:18). But they aren't looking for a miracle. They want a badge, a piece of paper, something to make sense of who this guy is and what just happened and why on earth everything is in disarray.

Jesus responds by pointing them to a completely different temple: his own body, the very dwelling place of God: "Destroy *this* temple and in three days I'll raise it up" (2:19, italics added). In many ways, this story has little to do with the moneychangers or the Temple itself and everything to do with Jesus. It isn't a diatribe against the Jewish faith, but a caution against any institutional systems and structures that keep us from hearing God speak in our midst.

More than once in the life of faith, the Holy Spirit has moved in our churches, with us failing to respond because of rules and traditions. Sometimes as we follow Jesus Christ, we glimpse a new opportunity for ministry only to have that vision squelched by others. Sometimes the people we love dearly, and who dearly love us, disappoint us when it comes to new expressions of faith. From the inclusion of women in the ministry, to the welcoming of immigrant communities of faith, to the questions we wrestle with today over the role of gay and lesbian people in the life of the church, our systems can get in the way of the presence of God in our midst.

I am an institutional girl and I love my United Methodist Church. I have chosen to serve here and have no plans to leave. But, as Jesus turns over the tables in the Temple, I find myself wanting him to turn over some tables in my denomination that keep us from the real ministry of Christ in the world —including such things as unnecessary paperwork, inflexible constitutions, timelines that are out of sync with the world, and standards for ministry that have little to do with the lifelong transformation of a single person. If all of those things were transformed so as to better support ministry, we all would benefit.

What is most important to discover in this Scripture passage is that God does not dwell within the boxes we have created; God desires far more than ritual and rules. Even with the Temple disrupted, Passover still took place.

People still found ways to praise God and to remember their history. It wasn't the building that was important; it was their relationship with God and their living faithfully according to his will. And the same is true for us.

Many years ago, Farmers Chapel United Methodist Church in Indianola, Iowa, was set on fire by an arsonist. The 107-year-old building was destroyed, and its people had to decide how to move on and how to forgive. Their pastor wrote a letter to this unknown person and sent it in to the local newspaper. It contained a simple request: "Join us for worship." It was an invitation for the individual to come and to experience forgiveness and love.

The presence of God does not dwell in our institutions or structures or buildings, but in the people of God through the grace of Jesus Christ. And when we open our lives to trust the Lord, we never know what might happen.

What are some structures and traditions of your church that Jesus might want to overturn?

1. From *The New Interpreter's Bible*, Volume I (Abingdon, 1994); page 830.

2. From the song "Won't You Be My Neighbor." Lyrics by Fred Rogers, in *The World According to Mister Rogers: Important Things to Remember* (Hyperion, 2003); page 142.

3. From *The World According to Mr. Rogers*, page 143.

4. From *The New Interpreter's Bible*, Volume I (Abingdon, 1994); page 850.

5. From "Moving On Up," The Pew Charitable Trusts (2013). *http://www.pewtrusts.org/en/research-and-analysis/reports/0001/01/01/moving-on-up*.

6. From "Lifetime Earnings of College Graduates," Pew Research Center (2011) by D'Vera Cohn. *http://www.pewsocialtrends.org/2011/05/16/lifetime-earnings-of-college-graduates/*.

Either/Or

Scriptures for Lent:
The Fourth Sunday
Numbers 21:4-9
Ephesians 2:1-10
John 3:14-21

In the now-ended ABC show *Lost*, survivors of a plane crash end up on an island. As they start to make themselves at home, one passenger, John Locke, sets up a backgammon board. Explaining the game to a boy named Walt, Locke holds up a black and a white counter and says, "Two players, two sides, one is light, and one is dark." This theme of light and dark, symbolizing good and evil, flows through the whole television series. Constantly, viewers are trying to figure out which side the characters are on. A similar battle between light and dark is present in our lives, too. Our need for salvation places us on the opposing team from God. The question is, how do we switch sides?

That struggle between life and death, good and evil, light and dark, fills our Scriptures. The Israelites must decide if they are going to look backward towards death or trust God and enter the Promised Land. Ephesians contrasts people of this world with those who share the exaltation of Christ. John's Gospel separates those who love the light and those who love the dark. There is no in-between. Salvation is happening with or without us.

The past must give way to the future. The power of sin is no match for the power of Christ. Death stands no chance when confronted with life. With endless mercy, love, and grace, our Lord invites us to step out of the darkness and become people of the light. But it is just that, an invitation. Will you accept the gift of salvation?

CHANGE OR DIE
NUMBERS 21:4-9

In a world of rapidly changing technology, many companies and industries are faced with a dilemma: They must adapt or they will die. Blockbuster, Borders, Kodak, and others have all failed to look toward the future and were caught in business models that did not meet the changing preferences of customers.

Thom Schultz, founder of Group Publishing and Lifetree Café, wrote about Kodak in particular and what the church can learn from its story. He tells how the brand was the first to invent the digital camera in 1975. However, they believed they were in the film business, shelved the idea, and hoped no one would notice. As digital cameras exploded on the marketplace in the 1990's and they lost market share, Kodak refused to change, afraid of losing what little they had.[1]

I see in the struggle of the Israelites a parallel to Kodak's story. For forty years, the Israelites have been wandering through the wilderness. Now they must finally decide if they are going to continue looking back toward Egypt or if they will trust God and enter the Promised Land. God has saved the Israelites from the oppressive hand of Pharaoh, led them to freedom through the sea, and guided them day and night. Through Moses, they've been told about the future that awaits them. Like the people of Kodak discovering a technology that would revolutionize everything, they've found the key to salvation but aren't quite sure how they feel about it.

Like us, the Israelites are human. They keep thinking back to the days when they were dependent upon Pharaoh: when a hard day's labor earned them some bread; when they were stuck in a system of injustice, but at least they knew what to expect; when the only thing they had to rely on was their own two hands. You know, the good old days of hell.

Our passage comes at a moment of transition for them. They find themselves in the middle of nowhere, utterly dependent upon God, faced with the deaths of their mothers and fathers and leaders. The first generation of those who had been rescued from Egypt was nearly gone; even Miriam and Aaron had recently died. Would the present generation of Israelites die in the wilderness as well, or would they take up the call of God to find shalom? We can cling so firmly to the past that we can't see the future right in front of us.

Margaret brought her King James Bible to my Bible study every week. She'd received that Bible as a third grader and it was the only one she'd ever owned. In her view, it was the only translation of the Scriptures that counted. But, she couldn't understand the words on its pages. This dear soul struggled with it because she read only at the seventh grade level. One day, Margaret admitted to me that she was holding on to that beloved Bible, but she didn't know what it said about Jesus. Like Kodak, stuck in film instead of focused on images, she was stuck with the antiquated words and didn't know the *Word*.

"Why did you bring us up from Egypt to kill us in the desert, where there is no food or water. And we detest this miserable bread!" shout the Israelites

(21:5). Complaining about manna and looking back to, well, who knows what they were looking back to, the Israelites forget they are only where they are by God's grace. Their liberation? The miracles in the desert? Their very survival? None of that happened by their own effort. It was all God. It was all grace. It was all around them. As the idiom goes, if it were a snake it woulda bit 'em.

And it did. The Lord sends poisonous snakes to the people because of their doubts and grumbles and complaints. If you look at the Hebrew word translated here as "poisonous snakes" you'll find the word *seraph*. The same word describes the winged creatures in the temple of Isaiah's day (Isaiah 6:1-7). In either place, when someone encounters the seraph, the person is moved to confession. Isaiah cries out, "Mourn for me; I'm ruined! I'm a man with unclean lips" (Isaiah 6:5). The Israelites cry out, "We've sinned, for we spoke against the LORD and you" (21:7).

In both cases, however, the seraphs become a source of healing and restoration. One removes Isaiah's sin (Isaiah 6:7), and one becomes an instrument of healing in Numbers. God commands, "Make a poisonous snake and place it on a pole. Whoever is bitten can look at it and live" (21:8). And in both places, the seraphs represent a turning point in the lives of those who meet them. Isaiah begins his prophetic ministry after this experience. The Numbers account is the last of the stories of murmuring among the Israelites. From now on, they keep their eyes focused on the Lord and prevail. They choose to let go of the past. They choose to live into a new future, with God leading the way.

In my Bible study with Margaret, we often took turns reading a passage and then discussing it, but Margaret kept passing when it was her turn to read. As someone else would read aloud, you could hear Margaret mutter under her breath, "Huh! So that's what that means." Eventually, Margaret agreed to explore some other translations, and we went together to our church library. When she picked up a translation more appropriate for her reading level, an entirely new world of the Scriptures opened up. She found the living Jesus on the pages of her new Bible; it spoke to her, made sense, gave her hope for her life.

Not so for Kodak. Schultz writes that Kodak was "clinging to what worked in the past at the expense of embracing the future . . . [the company] failed and squandered tremendous opportunities because its leaders chose to defend the status quo."[2] Over and over, we murmur about our present, and we cling to the past when what we really need to do is discover the future God has in store for us.

Where are you looking back?
What do you refuse to change? Why?

LIFE OR DEATH
EPHESIANS 2:1-10

One of my favorite books is *Hope for the Flowers*. In it, a little caterpillar named Stripe is looking for something, but he isn't quite sure what. He was happy for a while, but now he is restless. He knows there is something more out there. One day, he comes across this mound, this heap, this mountain of other caterpillars. They are all climbing on top of one another, trying to get as high as they possibly can. There are rumors of something wonderful at the top of the pile.

Stripe joins them. He is yearning for what is at the top, even though he doesn't know what "it" is. And along the way, he makes some terrible choices. He hurts others. He pushes them out of the way. He has to stop looking in their eyes so he doesn't feel so bad about what he is doing. Ephesians tells us about the "people of this world . . . [who] followed the rule of a destructive spiritual power" (2:2). Stripe was looking for life in the midst of the dead. He was looking for life among things that were actually sucking the life right out of him.

For one of my good friends, John, a similar destructive spiritual power marked his career. For years, he had worked in the corporate world and built his own company. He climbed toward the top, seeking success and power and telling himself that when he got there, he could enjoy life. But when he got to the top, John only found a longing he couldn't quite fulfill.

While I was in seminary, I saw in action a powerful ministry called Magdalene. It was founded in 1997 by Rev. Becca Stevens. That ministry works to address the "forces that drive women to the streets." Women who come to Magdalene have lived hard lives, many having experienced sexual abuse, growing up with drugs or alcohol, having been in and out of prisons, and/or selling their bodies on the streets. They are trapped by addiction, trauma, and "a culture that continues to buy and sell women."[3]

Hell can be addiction. It can be a force of destruction that leads us to crave the next big win or high. We use up our money and influence and relationships. Sometimes hell is more subtle. My friend John's life appeared to be going well, but sin is anything that stands in the way of God's intent for this creation, the shalom of the world. It is anything that puts a barrier between your life and the "good things" we were "created in Christ Jesus" to do (2:10). Ephesians suggests that although we are intended for these good things, we often cannot see them. We are trapped in sin, subject to the spirit of disobedience. Hell is what we know and what we desire. We are swimming in the powers of this world unawares. Like Stripe, we are stuck in an endless climb of despair and defeat, and we don't know any better.

But one day, Stripe sees something that nearly makes his heart stop. He sees a butterfly. He's been keeping his head down, not looking at anyone or anything when he catches a glimpse, a possibility of something he can't quite comprehend. In Ephesians, there are the dead and there are those who have been "brought . . . to life with Christ" (2:4). By God's grace, we catch a glimpse of the great love of God in Christ Jesus. By God's grace, we come to understand that "we are God's accomplishment" (2:10), a new creation, wonderfully and carefully made. By God's grace, we can be saved.

It happened that John went to church one Sunday and the Holy Spirit moved him. He caught a glimpse of another life that awaited him. He went home and put his business up for sale and enrolled in seminary. John was completely unaware of what God had in store for him, but he knew that everything needed to change. Similarly, the Magdalene program offers a new start to women who "have survived lives of prostitution, trafficking, addiction and life on the streets."[4] A two-year residential program provides counseling and recovery while the ministry's social enterprises (Thistle Farms and Thistle Stop Café) offer job opportunities and skill building. All along the way, graduates of the program who continue to be involved guide the way. But it takes the personal dedication of each woman to imagine a different life for herself and by God's grace to claim it.

Stripe decides to climb down from the pillar and everything that he knew. He sees another caterpillar, far away from the piles of caterpillars climbing to the sky. She makes a spot on a branch and wraps herself in a cocoon. Stripe senses her calling out for him to join him. So he finds his own branch and builds a cocoon. He dies to the world as he knows it, and on the other side of that cocoon, he finds a radically new life as a butterfly. Ephesians also describes a radically transformed life. Everything becomes different:

That destructive spiritual power of this world? Gone.
The sin that held you back? No more.
A life where our whims carried us to and fro? Demolished.

Our life as caterpillars is no more. Stripe was looking for life in the midst of the dead. But then new life found him. Ephesians makes clear that there is nothing we do to earn our salvation, and it's not something we previously possessed (2:8-9). But salvation is what God wants for us. This is God's gift to us. This is God's plan for our lives.

And more often than not, a community surrounds us as we take a leap of faith to accept that gift. Stripe followed the lead of a fellow caterpillar. John had a church that nurtured his faith and a family that stood by him, even as he turned their lives upside down. For the women of Magdalene, an outreach program offers hope, and the residents follow a rule of life with one another. The church itself is that place of support and nurture where we learn to lay aside the powers of this world and embrace God's shalom.

One of the interesting things about Ephesians is that it does not separate the newness of life we experience in our conversion from the "eternal life in heaven." In this letter, when we accept the mercy of God in our lives, we are brought to life with Christ, raised up with Christ, and seated in the heavens with Christ. The moment we step out of that cocoon, we are no longer caterpillars. Today, we get to be a new creation. Today, we are exalted with Christ.

And we have the courage to do so, because we have already seen butterflies. We have the faith to trust in God and let go of our baggage and old ideas and ways of doing things because we have seen God's amazing and transforming Resurrection power. We are the "future generations" that have witnessed "the greatness of his grace" (2:7).

What destructive spiritual powers are or have been present in your life? How has a spiritual friend helped you find life?

UP OR DOWN
JOHN 3:14-21

"God so loved the world that he gave his only Son, so that everyone who believes in him won't perish but will have eternal life" (John 3:16).

That verse is waved around at sporting events, put on bumper stickers, and is often used to summarize the entirety of the Christian faith. But it is far more complex than it appears. We cannot fully understand this verse if we take it out of context from the conversation Jesus had with Nicodemus, or for that matter, from the larger argument John makes in his Gospel.

John paints a picture of salvation by contrasting two pairs of opposites: up and down, light and dark. Both take us all the way back to the beginning— of both the gospel and the entire creation. First: up and down. In John's understanding of the universe, the heavens really were above our heads and the created world was below the heavens. But even if scientific discovery has shown us that the world is round, we can still use these terms to describe the flow of energy and life in John's Gospel. *Up* in this sense means to be with God. *Down* is life outside of the presence of God.

Second: light and dark. Light, in John's Gospel, is what gives us life and reveals truth. More often than not, John interchanges the words life, light, and the Word, using them all to point to Jesus. In the first chapter of John alone: "In the Word was life, and the life was the light for all people" (1:4).[5] The darkness, in contrast, is the force that opposes the life of God. It is the power that pulled the hearts of the Israelites back to Egypt and the spirit of disobedience Paul referred to in Ephesians 2:2.

John sets the stage "in the beginning" (1:1) with God and Jesus above (up) as the source of all life and light. The world, in contrast, is below (down) in the realm of darkness and death. Even though the world "came into being through the light" (1:10), the darkness is strong there, and people cannot see the light. Though we were created by God, sin, darkness, and death have blocked our vision. But, John tells us, God's intention for us is something more. Shalom is life and light in God's presence, and God acts to restore us. Jesus comes down to the world and lives among us. He brings light to the darkness (1:11). Then, Jesus is lifted up so that we might be lifted up, into the unending presence of God (3:13-15). It is only Jesus, the Human One, who can move between what is above and below (heaven and earth). When he does, heaven and earth are brought together and salvation is realized.[6]

With that bigger picture, let's go back to the conversation between Jesus and Nicodemus. Nicodemus has been living in the darkness (he even comes to Jesus under the cover of night). To understand their conversation about being "born anew," it helps to know that the underlying Greek word for "anew" can also mean "above." Jesus is trying to help Nicodemus understand that as long as he is down in the darkness of hell, he cannot understand the truth. He needs to believe in (have faith in and trust) the light and life that comes from above.

Then, in verses 14-15, Jesus points back to the reading from Numbers, where the snake on the pole brings healing only because it brings our attention back to God. In the same way, Jesus, the Human One, is lifted up. This "lifting up" of Jesus includes the entire act of his crucifixion, his resurrection, and his ascension. There is no separation between these moments, and in them, we see the light and come into the saving presence of God.

Finally, we come to that familiar verse. Out of God's great love for us, Jesus came down so that this "lifting up" might occur. When it does, those who see and believe will "go up" into the presence of God. For us, it all boils down to a simple question, the same question we have asked many times in this study: In light of Jesus' death, resurrection, and ascension, will you have faith in the One who brings life from death and light from darkness? It is not a judgment pronounced from on high; it is a decision we must make.

That reminds me of a conversation between Neo and Morpheus in the 1999 film, *The Matrix*. The premise of the movie is that all of our life is a dream, a constructed reality (the matrix) that conceals the truth from us. We are plugged in to a vast network and being used as human batteries. A renegade group seeks to wake people up from this fantasy to live their real lives. The movie is full of themes we can characterize as Christian: love and sacrifice, the need for rebirth, and what is possible when we believe.

In the film, Neo is still plugged in to the matrix, but he can sense something isn't quite right. He's inquisitive and makes an effort to find out what's going on. Nicodemus is also plugged in. He's one of the world's creatures, living in darkness. But we get the sense he, too, is searching for answers. Morpheus is a guide who offers Neo a choice between two different pills: red or blue. The blue pill will end their conversation, and Neo will remain in the matrix. His life will go on as it has before. But the red pill will allow him not only to discover the truth, but also to wake him from his slumber into the real world. Neo must decide if he will trust life as he knows it or place his faith in the unknown and impossible.

It is the choice between the darkness and the light. It is the choice Nicodemus faced standing in the shadows of the night talking with Jesus. The text does not give us Nicodemus' response to Jesus' teaching, and we might assume he chose to stick with what he knew and stayed in the dark. Yet when we look at the whole story John tells, we find Nicodemus no longer hanging out in the night. He steps into the public view, in broad daylight, after the Crucifixion and asks for the body of Jesus. He and Joseph of Arimethea want to bury his body (John 19:38-42). As Gail O'Day notes, Nicodemus leaves the secrecy of night and without fear steps into the light because of the crucifixion of Jesus. It is when Jesus is "lifted up," that the "moment of judgment" comes for Nicodemus and for Joseph, who had been keeping their faith quiet.[7] They step out of the darkness of below and into the brilliant presence of God.

When did you first encounter the lifted-up Jesus? Were you first drawn to Jesus' cross, his resurrection, or his exaltation?

1. From "The Church's Frightful Kodak Moment," Holy Soup with Thom Schultz, by Thom Schultz. *http://holysoup.com/2014/01/15/the-churchs-frightful-kodak-moment* .

2. From "The Church's Frightful Kodak Moment," Holy Soup with Thom Schultz.

3. From "About Magdalene," *http://www.thistlefarms.org/index.php/about-magdalene.*

4. From "About Magdalene."

5. From alternative translation of this verse suggested in CEB 1:4 note a.

6. From *The New Interpreter's Bible*, Volume IX (Abingdon, 1995); page 551.

7. From *The New Interpreter's Bible*, Volume IX (Abingdon, 1995); page 835–836.

Outcasts and Outsiders

Scriptures for Lent:
The Fifth Sunday
Jeremiah 31:31-34
Hebrews 5:5-10
John 12:20-33

In an episode of NBC's *The Office*, everyone gathers at church for the baptism of Jim and Pam's daughter. Everyone, that is, except Toby, the one who doesn't fit in with the others at work. He has to enforce rules and regulations, and the boss makes him uncomfortable. He's not the most social guy in the world, so you imagine he might be somewhere else that day. But then, there is a shot of Toby standing outside the church doors. Overhead, carved in stone, it reads, "All Are Welcome," but Toby can't bring himself to go in. Toby's life has been hell. He's been through a divorce. He struggles to have a meaningful relationship with his daughter. No one sticks up for him. Pam, the woman he loves, is inside that church, with her husband, baptizing their daughter. Toby is an outsider and he feels like God has cast him aside. That sign doesn't apply to him.

Many things can make us feel like outsiders, as if we no longer belong to a community and are no longer in the presence of God. We bring some of these things on ourselves through willful disobedience and sin. We can, for instance, be lazy and stop participating in the life of faith. Some of these things happen to us; illness and disability can exclude us if the community doesn't come to us or help us participate. Sometimes we find that if we don't look or talk or think similarly to others, we are not made to feel welcome.

Toby doesn't feel good enough, worthy enough, or loved enough. When he finally walks in the doors, long after everyone has left, he goes to the foot of the cross and asks, "Why do you have to be so mean to me?" In our Scriptures this week, a cry such as Toby's might have been uttered by the people of Judah, exiled for their sins and now under the rule of Babylon. It might have been uttered by sinners and lepers and the unclean, needing the intercession of the High Priest. It might have been spoken by the Greeks, who were not part of the covenant of the Jewish faith, but were trying nonetheless to catch a glimpse of Jesus.

The salvation of God brings the outcasts and outsiders into the community of faith and into communion with the Lord. God reaches out in love to provide everything we need to find our place, our home, our shalom.

FAILURES
JEREMIAH 31:31-34

Four years ago, I was absolutely set on learning how to play the guitar. I wanted not just to learn a skill, but to be able to play in my church for worship. I went to the music store, found the perfect instrument, and bought it on the spot. My brother-in-law Christian plays, and he offered to teach me, so we worked out an arrangement where he would give me a lesson each week when we came over for dinner.

For the first few weeks, I practiced every night. It was exciting to hold the instrument in my hands and hear the intonation of the strings. Eventually, however, I let other matters of my life take priority, and my practicing suffered. I began to dread my weekly lesson and on a few occasions, I conveniently "forgot" to bring my guitar to dinner. I was terrible at playing and eventually stopped trying.

We could easily substitute *obedience* or *prayer* or *service* for my guitar lessons. When we start on the journey of Christian faith, we are eager and so full of energy until we let other things take over. If we do not give our relationship with God the care and attention it needs, before too long, we discover our faith is sitting in the corner, gathering dust like my guitar, rather than being an active and vital part of our lives. Maybe it's because we are lazy or too easily swayed by the ways of this world. Maybe it's because we are weak. Each of us seems to have in our nature an inability to follow God fully—at least not instantaneously—the way that we want to or the way God desires us to. Call it what you want—the consequences of free will, original sin, or the brokenness of humanity—but there is something that seems to prevent us from fully accepting and embodying the will of God in our lives.

Our failure is not unique. Over and over, our spiritual ancestors struggled in their faithfulness to the Lord. In the midst of one of those times when the people of God seemed irredeemable, God called a prophet named Jeremiah. Jeremiah had some tough words for the people of God. He spoke harshly against their worship of other gods and their mistreatment of the poor. He told them that God was about to fall upon them. Before too long, the things Jeremiah spoke of began to happen. The king was taken away, the army collapsed, some citizens were taken into exile, and the temple was ransacked.

The people of God felt isolated and abandoned. But, in the midst of their despair, God told Jeremiah to set aside the words of judgment and condemnation and proclaim a message of hope: "The time is coming, declares the LORD, when I will make a new covenant with the people of Israel and Judah. . . . I will put my Instructions within them and engrave them on their hearts. I will be their God, and they will be my people" (31:31, 33).

Similar to the chords printed on the pages of my guitar music, the "Instructions" are God's words, meant to guide our actions and help us to live in holy relationship with one another and our Lord. But try as we might, we can't just pick that up all by ourselves. With only the good intentions of our hearts and minds and wills, living perfectly by those instructions is an unattainable goal. None of us, no matter how much we love the Lord, can do it on our own. Something must change, God says through Jeremiah. The Law is transformed from an external measure we must live up to into a relationship God writes on our very hearts.

The new covenant God promises is not a heart transplant, but a restoration. It is a continuation of the covenant made with Noah and Abraham and Moses, only this time God helps us fulfill our side of the relationship. An old Hasidic tale describes the stubborn nature of our hearts and need for this transformation: A disciple asks a rabbi, "Why does the Torah tell us to place these words *upon* our hearts? Why does it not tell us to place these holy words *in* our hearts?" The rabbi answers, "It is because as we are, our hearts are closed, and we cannot place the holy words in our hearts. So we place them on top of our hearts. And there they stay until, one day, the heart breaks and the words fall in" (italics added).[1]

Eventually, I went back to the basics and took the introductory guitar class at my local recreation center. I realized that as an adult who wants to do things right the first time, I need to be surrounded by beginners just like me. There were six of us in the weekly class, and our instructor gave us the same lesson he presented to elementary students. Slowly but surely, I am learning how to play. When we let go of our pride and our failure, our hearts break open, and the Word of God falls in. On my own, I won't get very far in learning to play guitar. I need instruction. I need encouragement. I need people around me who know just how much I want to play and who are willing to hold me accountable. But perhaps even more than those things, I need to remember that failure is part of the journey.

In the United Methodist tradition, we talk about grace in three ways. First, there is *prevenient grace* that comes to us before we even know who God is. Then, there is *justifying grace* that helps us to see what God desires of our lives. We come to understand what is required of us and see in the midst of our failures just how much God loves us anyway. And when we accept that love of God, the third kind of grace pours into our lives: *sanctifying grace*. That's what's engraved on our hearts to help us keep growing into the people of God each day.

Where does your heart need to break open?

DIRTY
HEBREWS 5:5-10

When my husband and I moved out of our first parsonage, we wanted to leave the place better than we found it. I am not the best housekeeper in the world, but I do try to deep clean before guests come over. In between, well, just don't knock on the door uninvited! I imagined that this last deep cleaning of the parsonage would be much like the scrubbing it got about once a month. We'd vacuum, mop the floors, clear away the dust, and be done.

Two days later, my knees hurt from scrubbing floors, my hands were raw from cleaning materials, and my neck had a funny kink in it from cleaning the corners of the ceiling and underneath the sinks. I couldn't believe how dirty the house was once all of the furniture was removed. I was surprised by how much dust had built up in those corners we don't usually see. The wear and tear of everyday use showed.

Our bodies and souls have their own wear and tear as well. We make mistakes. We fall down. We are used and abused. Terrible decisions affect not only our lives, but also those of others around us as well. We are unclean, and like our homes, we need someone to give us a good deep cleaning. When we talk about our sin, we often use the word *unclean*. Forgiveness of sin is about washing up. The Psalmist says, "Purify me with hyssop and I will be clean; wash me and I will be whiter than snow" (Psalm 51:7). Sometimes this unclean state is a result of our own transgressions, but it also comes because of our very humanity.

The problem with being unclean is that it separates us from the presence of God. It makes us unworthy to stand in God's presence—not permanently and not forever, but in that moment. One rule at my grandma's house was that you had to take your shoes off before you could come in. The grime of the world doesn't need to be tracked into God's house either. This often has carried over into the idea that we had to put on our "Sunday best" or "church clothes" when we came to worship the Lord. Times are changing though, and many today come to worship "just as they are" in the clothes they wear every day, be they jeans or khakis, flats or flip-flops. And as we are invited to make ourselves at home in God's presence, so Jesus comes into our unclean and messy lives and makes his home among us.

One role of the priest was to help clean worshippers up and get them ready to enter God's house. Ritual washing and sacrifice wiped away the scrapes and dirt from bodies and souls so people could make themselves at home in the Temple of God. This cleansing was itself a type of salvation, renewing, reviving, and welcoming worshippers into God's presence. People needed to go through these rituals repeatedly. Our homes get dirty from daily use, and so do our souls. Without the priest, people could not enter God's Temple, and even after the rituals, there was still some measure of separation between God and the worshippers.

The Temple in Jerusalem was destroyed in A.D. 70, just decades after Jesus was crucified, so the practices of the priests are not very familiar to us. The Letter to the Hebrews, however, is written to people who still remember the Temple, still look back to those practices, and are trying to make sense of their faith in Jesus Christ and the traditions of their ancestors. They wonder what their faith should look like without a priest to cleanse their souls. Where does God dwell without the Temple? Are we, today, left unclean and unworthy, cut off from God's presence?

In this Letter to the Hebrews, we find assurance that salvation is not only still possible, but has come once and for all in Jesus Christ. In answer to lingering questions, the author assures us that Jesus came to us "so that he could become a merciful and faithful high priest in things relating to God, in order to wipe away the sins of the people" (Hebrews 2:17). God's house is no longer a building of stone, but "we are his house if we hold on to the confidence and the pride that our hope gives us" (3:6), and God chooses to live in and among us.

Before, people were restored through ritual acts of forgiveness and cleansing, but the continual sacrifice of calves and goats and doves by the priests never made them completely clean. Now, they—and we—are washed in the blood of Jesus: "He doesn't need to offer sacrifices every day like the other high priests, first for their own sins and then for the sins of the people. He did this once for all when he offered himself" (Hebrews 7:27). Jesus Christ offers himself up as a sacrifice, both the high priest *and* the offering, to make us worthy of God's shalom once and for all.

In our specific verses from Hebrews for this week, we find Jesus fitting, in the words of Fred B. Craddock, "the twin credentials of a priest": Jesus is both "of the people" and "of God."[2] Priests who are "of God" are able to be faithful, and we can trust they are mediators of God's grace and speak with divine authority. Priests do not choose to do this job, but are chosen by God. In verse 4, the author of Hebrews points us to Aaron, the first priest of the Israelites, who served with Moses. And in verse 6, the author reminds us of Melchizedek, the very first priest named in Scripture, a holy king who blessed Abraham (Genesis 14:17-20; Hebrews 7:1-3). Jesus Christ is "of God" as well, "the light of God's glory and the imprint of God's being" (Hebrews 1:3). Priests also need to be "of the people" so they can relate to our struggles and deal with us gently in our unclean and sinful state. Jesus was one of us, lifting up prayers, crying out, even suffering as you and I do (5:7-8). Our God was not distant and aloof, but got down into the mud and muck of our lives to restore us to salvation.

Think of the love God has for us, coming to us and making such a difficult sacrifice to make us clean. No longer do we have to get ourselves right and clean and holy before we enter God's presence. Jesus comes into our unclean and messy lives and chooses to make his home among us, to restore us in his presence.

What is the state of your spiritual home? Are you ready for Jesus to do some spring cleaning?

WELCOME
JOHN 12:20-33

One afternoon, as Jesus was sitting with his Jewish companions, a few Greeks showed up to worship at the festival. They told Philip, "Sir, we want to see Jesus." This stirred conversation between Philip and Andrew, and together, they went to Jesus and told him. Why? Was there an issue here?

Their ethnicity made them different from Jesus' disciples. At minimum, their accents would have set them apart. These were Gentiles, outsiders. Would these gentiles be welcomed like children had been (Luke 18:16)? Would Jesus embrace the Greeks as he had sinners (Matthew 9:10)?

What might surprise us is that rather than words of welcome, Jesus responds to their entrance in the community by saying that it was time for "the Human One to be glorified" (John 12:23). He talks about his death and the need to lose one's life in order to live. He mentions a grain of wheat that dies in order to bear much fruit. His response includes this key idea, "My Father will honor whoever serves me" (verse 26). Later, he says, "I will draw everyone to me" (verse 32).

In the 2014 Sochi Winter Olympics, the Russian hockey team was expected to take gold. Their roster listed a number of star players, and the home crowd was cheering for them. But somehow, the team never came together. The Russians finished fifth overall and were knocked out of competition before they even got to the medal games. One of the greatest struggles this team faced was trying to combine players who had been stars in the predominantly American-based National Hockey League and the Kontinental Hockey League, based in Russia. Whether it was personalities or playing-style differences, the team never formed a cohesive whole. To represent their homeland faithfully, the players needed to join forces, but they failed to do so. Unable to set aside differences, each seeking his own glory, they lost. And that meant the hopes of many Russians for the Olympic Games were dashed as well.

In the same vein, our reading from John this week brings together two very different leagues of people. Gail O'Day says that the request of these Greeks to see Jesus "can be read as their desire to become disciples." She notes the juxtaposition of the very first Jewish disciples, Andrew and Philip, with these first Greek disciples (12:21-22).[3] They all want to seek Jesus and to follow him . . . but are they going to be able to get along? Will they be able to put their differences aside to form a cohesive team? Or will the past dictate their future as the Jews and Gentiles keep their distance and disrupt the hopes and dreams of salvation?

In that context, Jesus' apparent lack of welcoming words may not appear so surprising. We find instead a primer, for both Jew and Greek, about what true community and true salvation mean. Just as the Gospel of John has showed us before contrasts of light/dark and above/below, the parable of the seed is a contrast between a solitary life according to the ways of this world and a life of community according to the power of salvation. The Jews and Greeks can choose to remain seeds. They can cling to their sense of identity, loving life as they know it. If they do so, they will always remain strangers. They will keep their differences and never be lifted up with Christ.

But if they let go of their worldly identity and allow it to die, they will come to know true life in the new community of Jesus Christ. Jesus is asking them, and us, to declare allegiance. In doing so, we let go of the labels that have defined us in the past: Jew or Greek, male or female, young or old. We take on a new common identity as a servant of Christ. We come to define our community not by any reality of this world, but by the reality of Jesus' death and resurrection.

The single grain of wheat tells the story of salvation in Jesus Christ. It reminds us of the power of the Incarnation. In the dirt and the darkness of this earth, we live in difference and isolation. Just as we are, we will never experience the life, power, and presence of God. But as Jesus Christ entered this world, like a seed being planted, the power of salvation came among us. Jesus brought to earth the love that would transform us into the people of God. As Jesus entered our lives, he also entered our death. And as he was lifted up—on the cross and in his resurrection—we are able to enter into the presence of God and be lifted up as well. But we do so not in our difference, but as one people because of God's grace. O'Day describes this new community as "the fruit of Jesus' death; it is what shows forth Jesus' love to the world."[4]

Think of someone who appears or acts differently from you. In what ways can you get to know that person's story and learn how God has moved in his or her life?

1. From "The Broken-Open Heart: Living with Faith and Hope in the Tragic Gap," by Parker J. Palmer in *Weavings: A Journal of the Christian Spiritual Life,* March/April 2009, Volume XXIV, No. 2. Copyright 2008 by Upper Room Ministries, Nashville, TN; page 6. *http://ihmdonate.org/dotAsset/7abf3d9c-4c1e-42a7-9183-caf032459881.pdf.*

2. From *The New Interpreter's Bible,* Volume XII (Abingdon, 1995); page 57.

3. From *The New Interpreter's Bible,* Volume IX (Abingdon, 1996); page 710.

4. From *The New Interpreter's Bible,* Volume IX (Abingdon, 1996); pages 711 and 714.

ustice

Scriptures for Lent:
The Sixth Sunday
Isaiah 50:4-9a
Philippians 2:5-11
Mark 15:1-39 (40-47)

Lady Gaga's 2011 hit "Born This Way" got Rev. Brian Kirk thinking about youth ministry.[1] With lyrics like "I'm beautiful in my way / 'Cause God makes no mistakes,"[2] the song invites us to celebrate who we are, just as we are. For youth "who have been beaten down, oppressed, and made to feel worthless about themselves, the message that we are depraved and sinful creatures is not 'good news,' " Kirk says.[3] Kirk wants to offer these young people a church of love, not condemnation. The church has too often told young people what is wrong with them instead of inviting them in just as they are. The answer is affirmation and grace.

I wish Kirk had gone one step further, however, and called the church to repent. The love Kirk describes needs to include judgment or it fails to challenge the reality of sin. If this world were perfect, there'd be no violence or war, no oppression or hate. Sin is real. Those who suffer feel its consequences every day. We were born this way, too. The church needs not only to act differently toward these young people but also to challenge the social sin of the world. This time of Lent holds together the reality that we are both "fearfully and wonderfully made" (Psalm 139:14, NRSV) and that we all "fall short of God's glory" (Romans 3:23). We were born to love God and our neighbors perfectly. God didn't make any mistakes in doing this, but individually and as a whole, we have lost sight of that divine intention, and we have hurt and been hurt by one another.

The good news of the cross is that in Jesus' suffering, victims of this world find solidarity *and* justice. The cross is not to shame us with the weight of sin but to show us a path through sin to a new life in Christ and in relationship with one another. But this means we must be faithful and obedient to God's will. In God's shalom, people are never, as Lady Gaga's song says, "outcast, bullied, or teased."[4]

BUG BITES
ISAIAH 50:4-9a

I have never experienced harsh oppression or persecution. I was never bullied by my peers or had biting words aimed at me. But I have been bitten. I know what it means to say that "I gave my body to attackers," if not quite "my cheeks to beard pluckers" (50:6).

I have this comfortable, beautiful A-line skirt that I wear often in the course of ministry. It works perfectly with a black sweater or jacket and has a wonderful touch of femininity and reverence. For years, it was part of my "funeral wardrobe." One fall, I presided at a graveside celebration during the time of the soybean harvest. As family and friends gathered at the cemetery at the top of a hill, we could see out over fields being harvested and trees with the turning leaves of the fall. It was a beautiful and warm afternoon. But I quickly learned the dangers of the harvest. As combines made their way through the rows, dust flew everywhere. The commotion in the fields stirred up the millions of Japanese beetles that had been hiding among the leaves, feasting all summer. Now, there were beetles everywhere. I had noticed them around town but was completely unprepared for what we might experience of them at the graveside.

Although I was wearing a skirt, I had skipped the pantyhose because it was a warm day. We gathered around the casket for prayer, and the bugs began to attack. As I proclaimed the promise of resurrection, they landed on my bare legs. When I read Scripture, they crawled up under my skirt. As I tried to professionally preside in a solemn manner, those beetles bit everywhere, and it was all I could do to keep from screaming! During the prayers (when I hoped people's eyes were closed), I wiggled and squirmed to try to get some of those bugs off me. But for the most part, all I could do was stand there and take it.

In these verses from Isaiah, we find a "psalm of confidence" spoken by a faithful servant of the Lord. Faced with trials and tribulations, insults and attacks, the servant stands there and takes it. He knows that God is near and will bring help (50:8-9). The servant's ability to withstand the attacks comes from his deep trust in the Lord. In the context of the Book of Isaiah, these attacks are not necessarily random insults on an innocent soul. All of us have fallen short of God's intentions for our lives. The servant is one of many of the people of Israel, and the sin of the people has been growing and "feasting" for some time, like the beetles in the soybean fields. The faithfulness of the servant, however, is in contrast with some of the people who give up on God in the midst of their punishment. When the time of judgment comes, they must live with the consequences of their actions.

Typically, when we think of justice, we imagine people getting what they deserve—retributive justice that exacts appropriate penalty. We intend such punishment to deter offenders from committing crimes in the future. The harsh words of the prophet appear to be a call for justice, a warning of what will happen if they do not change their ways. But the prophet does not speak only warning and judgment; he also speaks of comfort and mercy. The time of exile will end and the people will return home to Zion. Yes, their sin led them into exile (50:1), but God is the source of both judgment and salvation. "Is my hand too small to redeem you? Don't I have enough power to save?" (50:2).

Grace and judgment are two sides of the same coin in God's act of salvation. Judgment allows us to let go of hell so that we can live into shalom. Christopher Seitz writes, "The fury of divine rebuke testifies to the energy God is prepared to expend to save."[5] We need to awaken and see that even in the midst of our sin and its consequences, God has not left us. In the midst of affliction, the servant of God trusts that "the one who will declare me innocent is near" (50:8). He perseveres, though he suffers, because of that hope.

Perhaps it would be better to think of a restorative kind of justice that seeks to transform a life so that relationships can be mended and a community can be made whole once again. When a woman named Susan shared her testimony about escaping an abusive marriage, I finally understood what that meant. She turned to her pastor for guidance, and he told her the right thing to do was to stay with her husband. If she left, he said, God would shut her out. In his church's teachings, her suffering was the will of God. In the kindest words I can manage, that pastor was *wrong*. Thanks be to God, Susan also called a friend and told her what that pastor had said. The friend asked, "You don't really believe that, do you?" They packed up her bags and she left.

If we return to Kirk's focus on grace, then God loves Susan and everything is okay. But Susan didn't feel okay. She was quick to point to mistakes she made along the way, though her mistakes in no way justified her husband's behavior. She found it hard to hear the hurtful words of people from her former church because their accusations resonated with what she had always been taught. She felt isolated and alone; yet she could not and would not return to the man who had been her husband or to the church she had loved. She knew that her experience of abuse had not been God's will, yet the aftermath of leaving felt like its own kind of hell. What would God's justice look like for Susan, both as a victim and as someone who felt complicit in a failed marriage?

Like the faithful servant in Isaiah whose ear was awakened by the Lord (50:4), Susan was awakened by God's grace; and in that, she found the strength to leave her broken marriage. And trusting in the Lord, she found the courage to withstand the fallout of that decision. She learned through wrestling with the change in her life that the One who would declare her innocent was near. When confronted by those who wanted her to justify her actions, she didn't hide her face or let herself be ashamed. Everything still didn't feel okay, but Susan learned that she didn't have to give justification for her actions: God was her justification. God declared her innocent, and God's grace had the power to transform her life. God would remain by her side long after those who condemned her moved on. On the other side of her trials, God has restored her to community: a new church family, a new and loving husband, and a life of service to the Lord.

In the midst of trials and tribulations, it's sometimes hard to see signs of God's presence. Yet like the servant in our reading from Isaiah, we should have a psalm of confidence on our lips. In our darkness and despair, God can transform our lives into light others might follow. At the funeral on the hill, being eaten alive by bugs, I wanted to scream and cry. I wanted to get back in my car and hide. But I looked around and saw others who were swatting beetles from their faces and their arms. I watched one or two crack a smile as I tried not to wiggle around. As soon as I concluded the service, the wife of the deceased man began to laugh between her tears.

In the midst of death, God brought sounds of joy to our lips. In the midst of judgment, there is always grace. Even if all we see around us is the dark hell of our sin, we can lean on God's promises, and find our way to shalom (verse 10).

When has God put a psalm of confidence on your lips?

UNDERDOGS
PHILIPPIANS 2:5-11

In 1887, a new term was coined in the English-speaking world: the *underdog*. This person is the opposite of the top dog, the opposite of the dominant person in a situation or hierarchy, the opposite of the winner, the opposite of the victor in a fight or contest of wills. The term likely comes from the world of dog fighting, but soon it was applied to politics, games, and life in general. Now we use the term underdog to talk about the one whom we expect to lose. The underdog is the one facing the uphill battle. Underdogs don't have the power, the money, the strength, or the system on their side. In an interview, playwright and poet Jessica Hagedorn summed up the nature of an underdog when she said, "I'm an underdog person, so I align myself with those who seem to be not considered valuable in polite society."[6]

Our Scriptures are full of underdogs: those who march into battle with nothing but slingshots to face giants, nothing but truth to confront kings, nothing but trumpets to demolish walls. Underdogs include prophets and apostles who don't stop preaching despite threats to their freedom and even to their lives. In Philippians, we find out that our Lord is an underdog. When he was born among us, Jesus gave up all of his "top dog" status and became one of us (2:7). Repeatedly, Jesus demonstrated humility. He reached out to those who were hurting and sick and those imprisoned by their sin. He invited them to the table and was mocked and rejected for doing so. He became vulnerable when he touched the unclean, welcomed children onto his lap, and spoke with a Samaritan woman. Christ was obedient to God's will, even when it meant death on a cross (2:8). Yet in that moment, God's very glory is shown. In giving up his status, in emptying himself, in this act of *kenosis*, Jesus reveals what divine power truly is: non-abusive, patient, never grasping, "power . . . made perfect in weakness" (2 Corinthians 12:9). From a jail cell, Paul encourages the Philippians to embrace that power, to embrace that love, to "adopt the attitude that was in Christ Jesus" (2:5).

Theologian Sarah Coakley argues that we should come to see the Incarnation and the cross as acts of "power-in-vulnerability."[7] Such a view reminds us that we are truly dependent on one another and on God. But they also remind us that the act of letting go of our will and living in obedience to God's will creates a powerful transformation in our lives. This power comes through dependence and relationship, through communion rather than a do-it-alone mentality. In Christ, we find encouragement and comfort, joy and love (2:2). To be in Christ means to live in a way that lets go of power in our own lives.

Sometimes, that means we need to seek out the underdogs of this world. Many underdogs live in the conditions of hell, pushed around and broken. In Christ, we need to stand with the widow and the orphan. In Christ, we need to not just minister to the poor, but also to get to know them, find out why they are poor, and work to change that. Our calling as disciples of Jesus Christ takes us into the dark and lonely corners of our community, to people who have no one, to reflect the light of God into their lives, even if it means that we put ourselves on the line.

As Kirk reminds us, the church has sometimes been an agent of oppression and injustice in this world. Historically, we have been on the wrong side of issues of slavery, justice for native peoples, and the inclusion of women in the pulpit. Salvation entails not only standing in solidarity with victims, but also acknowledging our role in perpetuating injustice and then letting go of our power. Throughout our history, there have also been countless people who have said, "No" to the institutions of injustice and who chose to stand with and for the excluded until they found a place at the table. I am utterly grateful for those who became underdogs for my sake. As we adopt the mind of Christ, our eyes begin to open to the underdogs we may have avoided or even have harmed. We each have a personal role and responsibility in those systems of sin that surround us. From the things we purchase to the food we eat, the very ways we treat one another are evidence of our participation in sin. When we act recklessly, others are hurt. When we ignore the cries of the needy, they suffer.

Coakley believes that to be in Christ, we need to practice discernment and contemplative prayer. In doing so, "we cease to set the agenda . . . [Instead,] we 'make space' for God to be God."[8] As we willingly humble ourselves, we set aside what we are entitled to, what we deserve, and instead discern the will of God and live our lives in obedience to it. That space also allows us to listen to the cries for justice all around us, to begin to see the underdogs in our midst. Prayerful discernment helps us to respond to injustice according to the love of Christ. In humbling ourselves, we find power-in-vulnerability. We find the strength and courage to act on behalf of those who can't. Whether they are immigrants or children with disabilities, grandparents who go hungry or single parents, Christ calls us to go and stand with them. Whoever they are, wherever they are, in Christ we are called to become underdog people.

Who are the underdogs in your community? How might you stand with them?

HELPLESS
MARK 15:1-39 (40-47)

"My God, my God, why have you left me" (15:34)? We could try to explain away these words of Jesus on the cross by looking at the fullness of Psalm 22, the opening line of which Jesus is quoting (compare Mark 15:34 with Psalm 22:1). The second half of the psalm is full of praise because God answered when the psalmist cried out. Yet when we sit with this chapter in Mark, we see only suffering. Jesus endures mocking, betrayal, violence, accusations, and death. Pheme Perkins points out that even if we are tempted to gloss over the struggle because we know Jesus will be resurrected, Mark forces us to experience the tension: "He saved others; he cannot save himself" (Mark 15:31, NRSV).[9] Why have you left me? Why have you forsaken me? Where is my help? The feeling of helplessness is terrifying.

In the fall, I sometimes help my dad move farm equipment from one field to the next. One cold afternoon, we had made three trips and just finished the last round of the day. But as we came around a corner on that quiet country road, we noticed what looked like a pile of clothes near the edge of the road. There had been a harsh wind all day, and anything could have blown into the weeds. Driving closer, however, we realized it was a person. We stopped the car and leapt out and into action. The woman was unconscious and warm to the touch. My dad called 911 as I tried to figure out if she was breathing. With the cold seeping in and realizing we had no idea what to do, that 911 call was our lifeline. But as seconds turned into minutes, I didn't hear sirens signaling help was near.

The woman began to wake, and we had enough sense to keep her from getting up and moving. We asked her questions and assured her we weren't going anywhere. But then she began to seize and drifted back into unconsciousness, and I started to panic. I had no skills to care for someone in a medical emergency. I had never taken CPR, and I was no longer sure she was breathing. Thankfully, emergency responders arrived shortly thereafter and gave her the care she needed. She survived and eventually recovered. Before they got there, however,

I felt as if my dad and I and this woman were the only people in the world. I feared she would die in my arms while I was completely powerless to help.

In the Passion narrative, I experience again that feeling of helplessness. I see it in the women who had followed Jesus but stood at a distance from the cross watching him die (15:40-41). They were helpless to stop his suffering. They could only be present, much as my dad and I were present on the side of the road. I hear echoes of my helplessness in the very words of Jesus. I find a Savior who suffers with me, not just for me. I can trust in this Savior who has been through "the darkest valley" (Psalm 23:4). He knows what it is to feel alone and forgotten, at the mercy of the circumstances.

But I also see my helplessness in the crowds who cried out for Jesus to be crucified (15:12-15). As I sat there by the side of the road, I tried to figure out if there had been something I had missed on one of those many trips back and forth along the road. Had she been there for hours and we hadn't noticed? We can point to religious leaders in the Passion story who force the crucifixion of Jesus, but there are unnamed crowd members and soldiers who play a part as well. They are complicit in his suffering. They invite us to think about how we have allowed ourselves to be swept along in sin without a second thought.

Take that cell phone I used to dial 911. We upgrade our phones for the latest model without paying attention. We think of technology as a disposable item that comes in a box from the store. But these devices contain rare minerals. Much of the tin used to solder together their parts comes from two little islands in Indonesia. The mining is done in thousands of shallow pits that cover the islands. Most of the extraction is done by hand as groups of males, often still boys, work in the muck, scraping the walls with their bare hands. Cam Simpson wrote about how dangerous the mining can be: "the walls literally just collapse and bury people alive. In one week . . . there were six men and actually a boy, a 15-year-old, who were buried alive in these pit collapses."[10] Our demand for smartphones has caused an industry to explode without regulation or safety. People are dying so I can have 3G.

The Gospel of Mark is a very fast-paced narrative. Jesus quickly moves from one thing to another. But in the Passion story, Mark forces us to slow down and experience the trial and crucifixion of Jesus. We find the religious elite fighting for power (15:1) and leaving innocent victims in their wake. We see how a few manipulate the will of the people, resulting in the casual sacrifice of the blameless (15:11). We see that words meant to dehumanize and mock the lowly lead to violence (15:17-20). We watch onlookers, some who taunt those who suffer directly and some who do so among themselves (15:29-32). Salvation not only takes away our sin; it brings into focus the experience of suffering. Justice can only begin when we are honest about our suffering and when we acknowledge the suffering of others. Salvation is for the innocent victim, the helpless bystander, and the perpetrators alike. And the cross of Christ is where they all meet.

I would never have known about my role in this sinful reality of tin mining had I not read that story. I am left with guilt that I am helpless to erase. At a conference in 2009, I heard theologian Jürgen Moltmann describe how he and his fellow Germans listened to the stories of survivors of concentration camps. He said that in the process, they learned "who we, the Germans, really were." Because of the Savior who suffered as they did, victims find the courage to tell the truth about their suffering. But salvation does not only affect the victims of injustice. Like the centurion (15:39), perpetrators can be transformed by the experience of another's suffering. In seeing how Christ died, the centurion was able to confess and believe.

When we accept Jesus as our Lord and Savior, we go to the cross where life and death meet. We have to pay attention to the reality of suffering. And we have to let it change our lives. Truth-and-reconciliation commissions are one model of this process; victims can tell their stories and perpetrators can acknowledge their role. I was powerless to stop a cell phone industry because I had no awareness of its sins. Now, I have the ability to make a conscious choice about my next technology purchase. Likewise, I was helpless to provide care for that woman on the side of the road, but her experience of suffering caused me to think about the training I can take so I can be equipped in the future.

When have you felt helpless? In what way have you been unknowingly complicit in the suffering of others?

1. From "Lady Gaga, Lent, Teens, and Original Sin," by Brian Kirk for *Patheos*. March 16, 2011. *http://www.patheos.com/Resources/Additional-Resources/Lady-Gaga-Lent-Teens-and-Original-Sin-Brian-Kirk-03-16-2011.html*.

2. From "Born This Way," by Lady Gaga, Interscope Records. 2011.

3. From "Lady Gaga, Lent, Teens, and Original Sin."

4. From "Born This Way."

5. From *The New Interpreter's Bible*, Volume VI (Abingdon, 2001); page 439.

6. From "An Interview with Jessica Hagedorn," by Jessica Hagedorn and Kay Bonetti in *The Missouri Review*, Spring 1995. Web. April 7, 2014. *http://www.missourireview.com/archives/bbarticle/an-interview-with-jessica-hagedorn/*.

7. From *Powers and Submissions: Spirituality, Philosophy and Gender* by Sarah Coakley (Blackwell, 2002); page 5.

8. From *Powers and Submissions: Spirituality, Philosophy and Gender*; page 34.

9. From *The New Interpreter's Bible*, Volume VIII (Abingdon, 1995); page 696.

10. From "Demand for Smartphones Takes A Human Toll Abroad," by Cam Simpson in an audio blog post for *All Things Considered* on National Public Radio, August 23, 2012. *http://www.npr.org/2012/08/23/159931391/demand-for-smartphones-takes-a-human-toll-abroad*.

Room at the Table

Scriptures for Lent:
Easter Sunday
Acts 10:34-43
1 Corinthians 15:1-11
Mark 16:1-8

The table is one of my favorite images of shalom— a great big table where all are invited, all are welcome, and all are loved. When we lived close to my in-laws, we made every Friday night our family night. We'd show up at dinnertime with a loaf of bread and dessert and feast on whatever my sister-in-law had prepared. The niece and nephews would set the table and argue about who got to sit by whom. As we waited for prayer time, the kids would sneak bites of food from the offerings on the table.

In the church, we gather for funeral dinners and church suppers around the table. Sometimes things are awkward. Sometimes we find ourselves sitting alone or on the fringes of a conversation or with silences we aren't quite sure how to fill. More often than not, though, when I sit down with people who are strangers, by the time we stand, we're acquainted. We talk about the food and how good the peanut-butter pie is. We share remembrances of the deceased. We ask about who someone is and where he or she comes from. We find moments of pure grace at the table. A youth connects with an older man who hasn't been in church for a few years. People mention their hurts and pains because they feel safe enough to share them. Grandma tells a joke and you laugh so hard milk comes out your nose. Especially when young and old, rich and poor, strangers and friends gather in one place, there is sometimes a sense that without this larger community, we are incomplete. We need one another. The table is incomplete—our lives are incomplete— unless they are there. There is a reason that we gather at the table. It's where stories are told and community happens.

As we celebrate Easter this week, we find three groups of people who have a story to tell. Each group has experienced the Resurrection, but the thing about God's salvation is that we can't keep it to ourselves. It's meant to be shared. So invite someone to the table, and get ready to pass the bread and share the faith.

WHO IS AT THE TABLE?
ACTS 10:34-43

Seventy-five years ago, I would not have been welcomed in most pulpits. As a woman, ordination would have been out of the question for me. A combination of tradition, a patriarchal society, and a particular interpretation of the Scriptures precluded the denominations now joined in the United Methodist Church from welcoming women as preachers and pastors. But today, I find myself in worship on Sunday mornings, robed and ordained, with my calling from the Holy Spirit confirmed by the church.

As a young woman, I have always been part of a church that ordained women. I have always been a part of a church that valued the contributions women made in ministry, in leadership, and in the world. It has been a given. And so it was a wake-up call to remember at General Conference in 2012 that my church has not always welcomed everyone. There, we celebrated the fortieth anniversary of the General Commission on the Status and Role of Women (GCSRW), which has worked tirelessly these past forty years to make sure women have a place in the church to lead and serve. We also celebrated full communion with African American Methodist brothers and sisters. Twelve years ago, we as a denomination first repented of our acts toward African Americans. The historically black Methodist denominations in our nation, beginning with the African Methodist Episcopal Church, were formed because of discrimination and exclusion. We now share sacraments and affirm the clergy and ministries of one another's denominations.

I think that it is important to have this backdrop of our own history of exclusion and discrimination as we explore our text from Acts. God had to prepare Peter to journey to the home of Cornelius, a Roman and a Gentile (Acts 10:1-2). Cornelius wasn't Jewish, but God was moving in his life. He actively supported the local synagogue and its ministries, even though he was not allowed into the temple to worship like those who were born Jews. In spite of his faith, he was not welcome at the table. God sent Peter visions symbolizing a new kind of family. Peter saw animals Jews considered "unclean" (10:10-16). As Peter was trying to figure out what it all meant, some messengers from Cornelius arrived (10:19). God was teaching Peter not about animals, but about people, and that there was room for more at the table of salvation. And Peter got the message. "You all realize that it is forbidden for a Jew to associate or visit with outsiders," he later told these messengers. "However, God has shown me that I should never call a person impure or unclean. For this reason, when you sent for me, I came without objection" (10:28-29).

Biblical commentator Robert Wall points out that Peter's role "is to proclaim salvation, not to dispense it."[1] Peter doesn't get to decide who is welcome at the table or where they sit; God does. God opens Peter's heart and mind, and Peter finally gets it: "I really am learning that God doesn't show partiality to one group of people over another" (10:34). As he testifies to Cornelius and his family, the Holy Spirit descends upon them (10:44). John Wesley, the founder of Methodism, was initially against women preaching and didn't want them behind the pulpit. But his job wasn't to dispense salvation either. When he witnessed the Holy Spirit working in the lives of women like Sarah Crosby, Grace Murray, and Hannah Ball, he relented and licensed them for preaching in the circuits across England.

The Book of Acts begins with the apostles in Jerusalem and preaching to Jews from all corners of the world who had arrived there (2:5). Then the message moves outward to Samaria (8:4-5). In our reading this week, the good news is proclaimed to Gentiles, and the family of God continues to expand. If the apostles in Jerusalem had been silent, if Philip had refused to go to Samaria, if Peter had not gone to Cornelius . . . who would have shared the story?

Because we are silent, there are still people missing from the table of salvation. There are still people who have never heard the story of the life, death, and resurrection of Jesus Christ. There are still people in this world who do not know that God loves them, or who feel excluded from our congregations. The signs outside our church buildings might say, "All Are Welcome," but are we willing to go into the homes of people who are different from us to share the good news? Do we actively let people know— with our words and our deeds—that they can enter this building and be a part of our community? Do we let the Holy Spirit lead us into the world to have new conversations and discover new friends?

The 2012 General Conference celebrated some ways we are reaching across the table, but we are still learning about what true repentance looks like in reconciling with Native Americans. We need acts of repentance to confess the ways we United Methodists have actively pushed our Native American brothers and sisters to the margins of society. As we experienced their stories and heard their suffering, I couldn't help but wonder whom we are excluding today. Where will we need to repent in the future?

May we have open eyes and open hearts and open minds to see the outpouring of the Holy Spirit in the lives of people in this world. May we always be ready and willing to share this church and this ministry with all of those whom God has chosen. And together, as friends of God, may we eventually all find a seat at the eternal table.

Who is still not welcome at the table? Whom is God urging you to invite to the life of faith?

WHAT IS YOUR STORY?
1 CORINTHIANS 15:1-11

When we go to dinner at my sister-in-law's house, there are a few table rules everyone follows:

1. Nobody eats before we pray.
2. You have to eat everything on your plate, or you don't get dessert.
3. Everyone has to tell three stories before they can leave the table.

Too often, the kids like to eat and then rush off to video games and dolls, so that last rule about telling stories keeps people at the table for quality conversation. Each of us is invited to talk about something that has happened in our lives so we can celebrate together, problem solve, or simply laugh. Like those gathered around my in-laws' table, each of us in the church has a story to tell as well.

The apostle Paul writes to the people of Corinth to encourage them in their faith and give some advice about problems and struggles that have arisen since he was last in town. When he gets to this part of his letter, Paul's main goal is to remind them of the foundation of everything he has taught: the life, death, and resurrection of Christ. That's the core of his message. That's the source of everything else he has said to them. The gospel is *the* story; the one that really matters. It is the foundation of their faith; it has transformed his life. "I am what I am by God's grace, and God's grace hasn't been for nothing" (15:10).

Bible commentator J. Paul Sampley believes Paul is calling back to the table those who have started to drift away from the message of salvation.[2] Paul is starting to worry about those in the family who seem to have believed in the gospel but now count it as "nothing" (15:2). He's thinking in particular about those who listened intently while he was preaching, but who have failed to "hold on to the message," who have not allowed the power of salvation to transform their lives. Some of the Corinthians still think they have to earn salvation. Some of them think they are unworthy of God's love and so don't accept it. Some believe that because they have lived a good life, salvation is already theirs. Thus, Paul writes blunt words meant to knock the cobwebs loose so these people might hear the story properly once again.

Although I am a pastor, some of my closest friends and family members have not embraced the gift of salvation. For some, the words went in one ear and out the other. Others want to do it their way and not God's. Some left the church at the first sign of hypocrisy and now want nothing to do with it. A few have always had it rough in this life and just can't accept, after everything that has happened, that God loves them. Each of us can probably name a person we would like to shake some sense into, someone we wish would come to know the gracious power of God's love. We feel this way, this aching in our hearts for our brothers and sisters, because we ourselves have experienced salvation's power.

The greatest story is a wonderful story, and it has a personal impact on us. The life, death, and resurrection of Jesus is woven into us who have experienced salvation. Just like my nephews and niece at the dinner table, we have stories to tell. Paul's testimony is not some bland witness about Jesus; it is the story of how the grace of God turned his life upside down and made something new. His words and his actions demonstrate that he is different because of the resurrection of Jesus. He stands on that promise and clings to it with every fiber of his being.

At the beginning of this study, we affirmed that we know who God is by what God does. What better testimony can you share about God than to tell others how God has acted in your life? Your story doesn't have to be dramatic like Paul's; it just has to be yours. You are not called to be a witness because you have a past, but because God has chosen you. We are alive because of Christ Jesus, not because of who we are. God works in the lives of all sorts of people. We find God through the murderer, Moses; the deceiver, Jacob; the prostitute, Rahab; the tax collector, Matthew; and the super-religious, Saul/Paul. But God also chose the farmer, Amos; the fishermen, James and John; the midwives Shiphrah and Puah; and countless other women and men.

In spite of our past or present, in spite of where we were born or to whom we were born, God reaches out with salvation and the invitation to receive that gift and stand firm in faith. Someone, somewhere once shared the good news with you. You heard their story and believed it. But as Paul begs us, not only do we need to believe but we also need to stand firm in that truth and shout it out with our own lives so that others may hear, too. Some of us have become "pew potatoes." Some of us are afraid to be sent into the community. Some of us are letting the good news sit on our shelves instead of sharing it with others. God is waiting to write the story of salvation on the hearts of parents with little kids, single dads, drug addicts, lonely residents in nursing homes, folks who partied too much last night, people who don't want to know Jesus Christ, and many more.

Don't let your gift of salvation be for nothing. God is waiting for you to bring someone to the table and tell them your story.

Think of a person your heart aches for. When was the last time you actually told that person how you felt? When was the last time you shared with that person why the gospel is so important to you? How might you do that now?

WHY ARE YOU AFRAID?
MARK 16:1-8

"Overcome with terror and dread, they fled from the tomb. They said nothing to anyone, because they were afraid" (Mark 16:8).

I reluctantly watch horror flicks with my husband, so words like *terror* and *dread* conjure up all sorts of terrible images in my mind. So I found it helpful to go back to the Greek and to look at the original words Mark used to describe the state of mind of Mary Magdalene, Mary, and Salome. The first word is *tromos*, which can be translated terror, but also trembling or anxiety. It is how you feel when something heavy weighs on your shoulders or you realize the enormous scope and power of something. The second term is *ekstasis*, and it relates to the word *ecstasy*. Like an out-of-body experience, a situation is so astonishing that we can't quite believe what's happening in front of us. Sometimes, the experience of having your mind blown is wonderful; sometimes, it's terrifying.

What the three women experience at that tomb fills them with trembling and amazement. That causes a line from an African American spiritual to echo through my mind: "Oh! Sometimes it causes me to tremble, tremble, tremble."[3] The Crucifixion, the burial, the long waiting during the Sabbath—all of these would have been moments of tromos and ekstasis for these women. But perhaps nothing could prepare them for the revelation of that morning. If you were there when the stone was rolled away, it might have caused you to tremble as well. Mary Magdalene, Mary, and Salome were left speechless by what they had seen and heard.

And that's how the Gospel of Mark ends. Jesus never shows up in his resurrected glory, there is no witness to the disciples, no sharing of the good news. Mark ends his account of the life of Jesus with three women, fleeing from the scene because they were overcome with tromos and ekstasis, and he tells us they said nothing to anyone. (Yes, there are more verses after verse 8, but most Bible scholars conclude that those were added later, by someone other than Mark. The oldest manuscripts of Mark end with verse 8.)

We, of course, can assume the women's silence about the empty tomb didn't last too long, and we can assume that for a couple of reasons. First, the other three Gospels tell us the women shared their testimony. All of them place Mary Magdalene at the scene, witnessing firsthand the resurrection of Christ and then sharing that message with the disciples. Second, if Mark's account is truly the end of the story, then how did we get here? If they didn't tell anyone, then how was the church born?

No, Mark has a reason for telling his story this way. Throughout the Gospel, Mark leads us on a journey, following in the footsteps of the disciples.

Every time the disciples make a mistake and behave like bumblers, we learn something more about who Jesus is. Each time they fail, we learn more about what it means to follow God. And this cliffhanger ending is no exception. Mark tells us the women were afraid and said nothing to anyone. We are invited to live the rest of the story ourselves. After we have encountered the holiness of God and the miracle of the Resurrection, what will we do? Will we let fear close our mouths? Will we roll the stone back in front of the tomb and conveniently forget that this all happened? Will we be silent? Or will we find the courage to risk it all to share this amazing and terrifying good news with the world?

Amazing and terrifying is a good description of what the gift of salvation is. We are filled with joy because the One who destroys all barriers comes to make us a new creation. Christ is risen! Jesus defeated death to give us life! The tomb is empty! Amen! But in the midst of that joy, there is also a healthy dose of fear—we would be foolish not to admit it—because with the empty tomb comes the amazing and awesome announcement that Jesus isn't dead. And if God is really out there—really present in this world that we live in, then everything changes.

A pastor in my conference, Rev. Bill Cotton, tells the story of a friend named Bob. "Bob was certain about three dependable things: Iowa's rotten weather, higher taxes, and the certainty of death." But if Christ has risen, death is no longer dependable. His friend Bob commented, "I was counting on death. Death is my way out. . . . If I can't count on death what's a guy like me to do?"[4] Indeed, what do we do when something we thought we could depend on is no longer true? When everything we know is changing and the world spins out of our control, tromos and ekstasis are common responses.

Control is the key issue there. In our spiritual lives, fear can arise when we come face to face with the holy and we are no longer in control. And any encounter with the holy rightly puts awe and trembling in our hearts. It's the kind of fear portrayed in C. S. Lewis' *Chronicles of Narnia* series, where the people rightfully fear and revere Aslan, the lion. He is dangerous. He is wild. He is wonderful. And the wild and wonderful Christ has risen from the dead and is calling our names. He has a word for us to proclaim.

We all have fears. I know they are there, percolating in your throat, ready to cut off the good news. So what better time than Easter to think about the things that overwhelm us with tromos and ekstasis? We fear speaking on behalf of others, because we are afraid to say the wrong thing. We fear seeking justice for the marginalized, because it might put us in danger. We fear telling the truth, because we might be rejected. We fear sharing our time and money with others, because there might not be enough. We fear welcoming strangers to the table, because they just might stay. And I think we fear all of those things because we haven't let ourselves fully accept the reality that Christ is alive. Not spiritually present, not a memory of the past, but actually resurrected from the dead.

And if Jesus really lives, then we don't need to worry about saying the wrong things, for the Holy Spirit will bless us with words. We don't need to worry about being in harm's way or being rejected, because we know that "nothing can separate us from God's love in Christ Jesus our Lord" (Romans 8:38). We don't need to worry about not having enough, because in the fullness of community we discover an abundance of gifts and resources that will sustain us (Acts 2:42-47). And we don't need to worry about the stranger, because Lord knows, we could use a few more bodies in our churches!

In his cliffhanger, Mark is, in effect, asking us a simple question: when—not if, but *when*—the terror and amazement of the good news seizes your life, what are you going to do?

When were you afraid to tell the good news of Jesus Christ? What would help you not be afraid in the future?

---

1. From *The New Interpreter's Bible*, Volume X (Abingdon, 2002); page 165.

2. From *The New Interpreter's Bible*, Volume X(Abingdon, 2002); pages 973-974.

3. From "Were You There," an African American spiritual.

4. From "Death is Undependable," by Bill Cotton, in *Thursday Memo for Preachers*, Easter 2009. *http://www.iaumc.org/enewsletterarchives/detail/396.*

eader Guide

HOW TO LEAD THIS STUDY

The Lord Is Our Salvation invites adults to explore and reflect upon the Revised Common Lectionary Bible readings for the season of Lent. This Lenten study is rooted in the texts for Year B of the three-year lectionary cycle of readings. Each week you will explore readings from the Old Testament (or New Testament history), the Epistles, and a Gospel. "How to Lead This Study" guides you in setting up and leading the study. You'll discover tips for preparing for each week's session, as well as ideas about how to successfully lead a Bible study, even if you have never led one before. Although the Revised Common Lectionary designates a psalm for each week, they are generally not discussed in the main content. These psalms, however, are listed in this section along with ideas for incorporating them into the session. "How to Lead This Study" offers some historical and theological information about the season of Lent and suggests ways that people now and in different times and places have observed this sacred time.

About Lent

As Lent begins we believers are called to recognize our mortality. As ashes are imposed on our foreheads in the sign of the cross, we squarely face the reality that we will return to dust and ashes. Lent is observed for forty weekdays, starting on Ash Wednesday. Actually, there are forty-six days from the beginning to the end of the season, but Sundays are always considered the Lord's Day and thus not counted in the days of penitence. During the season of Lent we are called to reflect on our sinfulness and our need to be transformed so as to be more closely conformed to the image of Jesus. Some Christians choose to give up something to focus more clearly on Christ. Following the pattern of the early church, many contemporary churches instruct youth and adults who intend to be baptized and/or confirmed during Holy Week. More seasoned Christians may engage in spiritual disciplines during this season that will be incorporated into their lives long after Lent has passed.

The Revised Common Lectionary draws together themes from the Old Testament, Epistles, and Gospels to help us make this Lenten journey. Although the readings vary, the three years share the themes of covenant and newness of life. The Scriptures read during Lent teach us that we can rely on God, who initiated the covenant. In turn, we are called to respond by obeying. We are offered new life in the cross, where we experience God's transforming grace. The Scriptures help us discern who we are and who we can become as we live in Christ.

Ways to Observe Lent

Certain traditions have surrounded Lent for centuries. Some Christians practice serious fasting during Lent. For example, Ethiopian Orthodox Christians fast from meat and dairy for eight weeks. On Easter Eve they attend a lengthy church service that often lasts until 3 A.M. Then they break their fast and celebrate the risen Christ.

Although many Christians give up certain foods during Lent, a British tradition features eating a special pastry on Good Friday. Hot cross buns are sweet breads flavored with spices and fruits. The top of the bun is iced in the shape of a white cross as a reminder of Christ's suffering. In Bermuda, hot cross buns are traditionally served with a sandwich of codfish cakes. Bermudians also play marbles and fly kites, particularly homemade ones created from sticks and tissue paper. According to local lore, the kites originated with a teacher who wanted to make a visual impression on his students concerning the ascension of Christ. Good Friday here is a day of celebration, with kite-flying events scheduled in many places across the island.

Some communities band together in an ecumenical crosswalk where Christians solemnly process from one church to another. Usually, someone leads the group by carrying a wooden cross. At each stop along the way, there is a brief liturgy, perhaps including a Scripture reading, prayer, and song. This walk is reminiscent of pilgrimages that were popular in Europe during the Middle Ages.

Lenten dramas are produced in some locales. Perhaps the most famous one is performed once each decade in Oberammergau, Germany.

Organize a Lenten Study Group

If your church has a series of short-term studies, this Lenten study can be added to the schedule either during the week or on a Sunday morning. If the congregation normally does not offer short-term studies, talk with the pastor and whichever committee is responsible for adult education about scheduling this seven-week study. As you think about scheduling, remember that typically a midweek study would explore the Scriptures for the upcoming Sunday, whereas a study held on Sunday would likely delve into the Scriptures for that day. If you want to do a study on a Monday or Tuesday, be aware that the first class will meet just before Ash Wednesday. Check the church calendar to be certain that the time you want to offer the study does not conflict with another event, such as choir rehearsal. Also determine which room(s) might be available. Before making a final decision, check with a few key people who are likely to participate to see how your plan fits with their schedules.

Publicity is important for such a study. Be sure that the time, date, room number, and cost of the study books (unless the church will offer these for free) are included in the write-up. State whether you wish to do preregistration, which is helpful for knowing how many books to order. Set a deadline for registration if you choose this option. Otherwise, state that all are welcome. Publicize this information through a variety of channels including pulpit announcements, bulletin announcements, church newsletter articles, church website, church social media, and community newspapers.

Decide what you will do concerning refreshments. Some light, healthy snacks might work on a Sunday morning. Offer participants the option of bringing a brown bag lunch to a midday session. Consider soup and sandwiches for an early evening meeting. Or, you may choose to have only beverages available and suggest that participants bring their own food.

Decide whether you want to hold a preregistration. Whether you do or not, be sure to order enough copies of *The Lord Is Our Salvation* so that each participant has the study book. The church will need to determine how much to charge participants or whether to underwrite the cost and announce that the study is free.

Prepare for the Sessions

Leading a Bible study is a sacred privilege. Before you begin the "nuts and bolts" work, pray for the Holy Spirit to guide you and the participants as you encounter each week's Bible passages. Try reading each Scripture devotionally by asking God to speak to your heart through a word or phrase that grabs your attention. Meditate on whatever you are shown and allow this idea to shape your own spiritual growth.

Read the Scriptures and Bible Background for each week's lesson to understand the context of the Scriptures and their meaning. If time permits, consult other commentaries to expand your knowledge. Once you feel comfortable with the Scriptures, begin to plan the session by following these steps:

1. Read the session plan from *The Lord Is Our Salvation*.
2. Refer to the Session Plan where you will find suggested activities

for each Scripture, as well as activities to open the session and close the session. Decide which of these activities will work best with your group. Be aware that the activities generally include discussion, but some include art, music, movement, or other means of learning in addition to discussion.

3. If you choose activities that refer directly to *The Lord Is Our Salvation,* mark the places in your book for easy reference during the session.
4. Gather supplies for the selected activities.
5. Select hymn(s) if you wish to use them. If you will sing the hymn(s), notify your accompanist.
6. Determine how you will use the lectionary psalm or other additional readings.
7. Contact any guest speakers or assistants early in the week if you will use their services.

Think about the comfort of the participants in the learning area. Since they will have study books, Bibles, and possibly notepads, your group may prefer sitting at a table. Check to be sure that heat or air conditioning, light, and ventilation will be adequate for the time of day you plan to meet. (Some churches thermostatically control heat, allowing it to come on only at certain times unless it has been reset.) Also be aware of those with impaired hearing or sight who may hear or see better in certain seats. Likewise, consider how difficult someone with a mobility issue will find it to get to the learning area and locate suitable seating. If the room is not accessible, see if you can be reassigned to a room that will accommodate a person who has physical challenges. Make sure that a small worship table and large writing surface, such as an easel with large sheets of paper and markers, a whiteboard with markers, or a blackboard with chalk will be on hand. Have a separate space available and a designated worker to provide childcare if necessary.

Helpful Ideas for Leading a Group

Bible studies come in many shapes, sizes, and formats. Some begin with a theme and find biblical support for it. Others begin with the Bible itself and unpack the Scriptures, whether from one book or several. Our study begins with the Bible, specifically the texts of the Revised Common Lectionary. Those Scriptures will deeply inform our study. However, *The Lord Is Our Salvation* is not a "verse by verse" study of the readings. Instead, we are studying the texts as a kind of road map to guide us in our spiritual journey through the Lenten season. Consequently, some of the suggested activities call participants to struggle with questions of faith in their own lives. Our focus is primarily on transformation so that participants may grow in their relationship with Jesus Christ and become more closely conformed to his image. That's a tall order for a seven-week study! And it may be somewhat challenging for the participants, since it may be far easier to discuss historical information about the Bible and consider various interpretations of a passage than it is to wrestle with what the passage says to us—personally and as members of the body of Christ—in contemporary life.

Your role as the leader of this group is to create an environment in which participants will feel safe in raising their questions and expressing their doubts. You can also help the class feel comfortable by making clear that you rely solely on volunteers to answer questions and to read aloud. If adults feel pressed to respond or read, they may be embarrassed and may not return to the group. If questions arise that you can definitely answer, do so. If you do not know the answer but suspect that an answer is available, say you do not know and offer to look it up and report back at the next session. Or, suggest a type of resource that will likely include the answer and challenge the questioner and others to do some research and report back. Some questions cannot be fully answered—at least not in this life. Do not be afraid to point out that people through the ages have wrestled with some questions and yet they remain mysteries. If you can truly say so, respond that you have wrestled with that same question and have found an answer that works for you, or that you are still searching. When you show yourself to be a co-learner, the participants will feel more comfortable than if you act as the all-knowing expert. You will feel more at ease about leading the group as well.

Additional Scriptures for Lent

Each week the Revised Common Lectionary includes a psalm. On the Sixth Sunday in Lent, two psalms are listed in the Lectionary, one to accompany the Liturgy of the Palms and the other, the Liturgy of the Passion. Since this study will focus on the Liturgy of the Passion, only that psalm is noted. You will find ideas for incorporating the psalms into the study in each session. Also consider reading the psalm responsively from a hymnal with a Psalter. Or, if your church tradition includes chanting, consider chanting the psalm. Some hymnals include dots over the words to indicate when the note should be changed. Many hymnals also include sung responses, which you may want to use.

First Sunday in Lent: Psalm 25:1-10
Second Sunday in Lent: Psalm 22:23-31
Third Sunday in Lent: Psalm 19
Fourth Sunday in Lent: Psalm 107:1-3, 17-22
Fifth Sunday in Lent: Psalm 51:1-12 or 119:9-16
Sixth Sunday in Lent (Palm/Passion Sunday): Psalm 31:9-16 (Liturgy of the Passion)
Easter Sunday: Psalm 118:1-2, 14-24

1. Keep Me from Drowning

BIBLE BACKGROUND

Water, which can give life but can also cause suffering and death, is a common image in the three readings for this week. Hence the lesson title, "Keep Me from Drowning." In Genesis 9, the story of the Flood concludes with God making a covenant with all creation that never again will a flood destroy the world. The Flood is recalled in 1 Peter 3:18-22 where the writer compares the rescue of Noah and those on the ark with baptism, which also saves. In Peter's Epistle, the Flood of Noah's day "prefigured "(3:21, NRSV) the baptism of those who believe. The Gospel reading from Mark recounts the story of Jesus' own baptism, which was followed by his temptation in the wilderness and his initial preaching in Galilee.

Genesis 9:8-17

The first readings during this Lenten season survey much of the Old Testament story. A key theme in most of these passages is covenant. That theme figures prominently in today's reading, which concludes the story of the Great Flood that began in Genesis 6:5. Seeing the evil that had come upon the earth, "the LORD regretted making human beings" (6:6) and determined to "wipe off of the land" (6:7) not only humanity but other living creatures as well. God vowed to destroy all of creation that God had once repeatedly recognized as "good" (Genesis 1:4, 10, 12, 18, 21, 25, 31). Only Noah, his family, and one pair of all creatures would be allowed to survive in an ark during this devastating Flood (6:18-21). After the waters had subsided, "Noah built an altar to the LORD" and offered sacrifices (8:20). Then God announced a unique covenant, one which would include not only Noah and "every future generation" but also "every living thing" (9:12). Moreover, as part of this covenant, God promised that there would never be another flood that would cause such global destruction (9:11).

God chose the rainbow as the symbol for this covenant with all life on earth. The Hebrew word used in verse 13 means both rainbow and bow. In addition to understanding this symbol as a natural phenomenon associated with rain, it also carries the meaning of a weapon. Only in Genesis 9 and Ezekiel 1:28 (NRSV) does "bow" refer to a colorful arc seen in the clouds. Elsewhere, such as in Lamentations 2:4 and Habakkuk 3:9, the bow is clearly an instrument of war used by both soldiers and gods, including the God of Israel. By choosing the bow with its double meaning as a symbol of this covenant, God is assuring all creation of peace with its creator.

Although most covenants call for an agreement on the part of all parties, this one is unconditional. It is the loving, gracious act of a God who refuses to give up on the world.

1 Peter 3:18-22

Suffering, and how to behave honorably in the face of it, is an important theme in the First Letter of Peter. Today's passage opens with the words, "Christ himself suffered on account of sins." The people to whom the letter was addressed were suffering "various trials" (1:6). Their actions or attitudes had not caused this suffering, but rather it was due to their loyalty to Christ and "righteousness" (3:14). This suffering would not last long before God would "restore, empower, strengthen, and establish" them (5:10). Yet in the midst of their tribulations, Christ's suffering served as an example for them (2:21). They could learn from him and entrust themselves to God, just as he had (2:23). Although believers were suffering for their faith in Christ, he had suffered on their behalf in order to set things right between them and God. His atoning death, unlike the sacrifices made in the Jewish Temple, occurred "once" and was "for all" (3:18). Jesus truly died "as a human" (3:18), but he was resurrected and brought to life by the power of the Holy Spirit. His Resurrection is what enables believers to be saved (3:21).

The water images of Genesis and Mark meld together in First Peter. The ark is mentioned as the source of salvation for Noah and his family, who were able to survive the raging flood waters. The rest of humanity, referred to as "disobedient" spirits (3:20), were visited "in prison" by the resurrected Christ (3:19). Verses 19-20 are enigmatic; they may indicate that Jesus preached to these spirits prior to his incarnation, in their own lifetimes during the days of Noah. Alternatively, these verses could describe Jesus' activity during the interval between his death and resurrection. In that case, Jesus descended to the dead and preached to these people, now long-dead spirits, of Noah's time. Whatever the interpretation, the central point seems to be that by the Spirit's power Jesus preached the good news even to these imprisoned, disobedient spirits.

In a further connection, salvation in the ark is also linked to water baptism offered by the church (3:20-21).

Mark 1:9-15

This brief reading from Mark includes three scenes from the beginning of Jesus' ministry: his baptism (1:9-11), his temptation (1:12-13), and his first public preaching (1:14-15). Mark's Gospel omits a Nativity story and opens with John the Baptist preaching about the one who was coming after him and baptizing in water those who were "confessing their sins" (1:5, NRSV). Jesus journeyed south from his home in Nazareth in the region of Galilee to be baptized by John in the Jordan River. Although the word *Trinity* is never used in the Bible, the Son, the Spirit, and a heavenly voice—typically interpreted as the Father—are all mentioned together here. At his baptism, Jesus saw the heavens opening and God's Spirit descending upon him "like a dove" (1:10). This dove may call to mind the dove that returned to Noah with an olive leaf, signaling that the waters had receded and bringing hope for a new creation (Genesis 8:8-12). In verse 1, Mark had announced that Jesus was God's Son; here in verse 11, the Father's voice affirms in Jesus' hearing that he is indeed God's Son.

As First Peter reminded believers, Jesus suffered. That suffering began in the wilderness, where the Spirit had "forced" (1:12) Jesus to go to be tempted by Satan. Unlike the accounts in Matthew and Luke, Mark does not give specific details of the temptations, but he does mention that Jesus' sojourn in the wilderness lasted forty days, the same amount of time that it rained during the Flood (Genesis 7:12). The wilderness was inhabited by "wild animals" (verse 13), some of which were thought to harbor demons (see Isaiah 34:14). In contrast to Matthew 4:11, which reports that angels came to care for Jesus after the devil departed, Mark 1:13 does not specify a time when the angels came.

John had been arrested before Jesus returned to Galilee to begin preaching. Jesus' message was brief but profound: The time has come for God's kingdom to break into human history. Turn toward God. Believe this good news.

SESSION PLAN

Open the Session

Welcome participants and attend to housekeeping matters, such as distributing *The Lord Is Our Salvation*, collecting money for the book, clarifying the time and place of future meetings, and pointing out restroom locations.

Mention that the title for today's session is "Keep Me from Drowning." Invite a volunteer to read the chapter's introductory section under this title.

Encourage participants to reflect silently on the following questions:

1. In what ways do I feel that I am drowning?
2. Where am I looking for help to survive?
3. What help am I hoping to find during this Lenten study?

Offer a prayer.

Saving God, in you and you alone I put my trust. You know the challenges I face. By your grace and mercy, keep me from drowning. Amen.

Engage the Scriptures

Analyze the story of the Flood.

Invite volunteers to recall why God decided to send a flood, what God commanded Noah to do, and what happened when the waters finally receded. See Genesis 6:5–9:17, the Bible Background, and the first three paragraphs of "The Rainbow" for reference.

Select a volunteer to read Genesis 9:8-17. Ask participants to listen in these verses for what God is going to do following the Flood. Discuss the following questions:

1. With whom is God creating a covenant?
2. What does God promise to do?
3. What does Noah have to promise, and how will that affect God's promise?
4. What is the sign of the covenant?
5. Why is this sign so appropriate? (See the Bible Background and paragraph under "The Rainbow" beginning with "In the ancient . . .")
6. What do you learn about God's intended relationship with humanity from this story and covenant?

Reflect on a rainbow bridge.

Gather candles in these rainbow colors: violet, indigo, blue, green, yellow, orange, and red. Set these up where everyone can see them. As alternatives, prior to the session create a rainbow using construction paper or find a picture of a rainbow.

Choose a volunteer to read Genesis 9:8-17. Select someone else to read the information under "The Rainbow," beginning with "This story of . . ." through the end of the section.

Distribute paper and pencils and invite participants to reflect on these questions by writing words and/or drawing pictures: Imagine yourself walking under this magnificent rainbow, the covenantal symbol of God bridging the gap between human sinfulness and God's peace with the world. What changes in your life will you ask God to help you make along your journey? What are you hoping to find at the end of your rainbow journey? Solicit comments from volunteers concerning any insights they gleaned.

Examine the relationship between suffering and salvation in First Peter.

Select a volunteer to read 1 Peter 3:18-22.

Form two teams. One will look at the Bible Background for the Epistle and "A Broken Cross'" for information about salvation. The other team will look at the same two resources for information about suffering.

Call the teams together and ask a spokesperson for each one to comment on their team's discussion.

Ask: If someone were to say to you, "I cannot believe that Jesus suffered in order to bring salvation," how would you respond?

Construct a cross.

Choose a volunteer to read 1 Peter 3:18-22.

Read or summarize the Bible Background for today's Epistle lesson.

Set out supplies that you have collected during the week. You may also want to ask others to bring supplies. Instruct the participants to make a cross using the supplies that have been provided. The cross could be a bookmark made of paper or construction paper on which participants write these words from 1 Peter 3:18: "Christ himself suffered on account of sins, once for all . . . to bring you into the presence of God." Natural objects, such as twigs or stones or leaves, could also be used to create a cross. So can recycled objects such as buttons or pieces of jewelry mounted on paper or fabric or craft sticks. Encourage participants to use their imaginations with whatever supplies are available.

Conclude this activity by reading 1 Peter 3:18 in unison and then suggest that participants place their crosses where they can see them daily throughout this Lenten season as a reminder that Christ died for them.

Study the beginning of Jesus' ministry.

Solicit three volunteers to read respectively Mark 1:9-11 (Jesus' baptism), verses 12-13 (Jesus' temptation), and verses 14-15 (Jesus' message). Note that the first two segments record Jesus' preparation for ministry, and the third segment challenges those who hear Jesus to change their hearts and believe the good news he brings.

Call on a volunteer to read from "The invitation to change . . ." through the end of "Now Is the Time," including the final two questions.

Distribute paper and pencils. Invite participants to write answers to the two questions. Mention they will not be asked to discuss their responses.

Encourage participants to review the questions and answers each day this week, and in doing so, open their hearts to greater change in response to God's good news.

Remember your baptism.

Choose a volunteer to read Mark 1:9-15 and invite comments on notable features of Jesus' baptism as a preparation for his ministry.

Encourage participants to tell stories of what they remember (or have been told) concerning their own baptisms. What made this event so memorable?

Provide an opportunity, in accordance with your faith tradition, for participants to remember their baptisms. Be aware that most denominations do not engage in rebaptism, because God's grace is sufficient the first time. However, services of remembrance of baptism may be in keeping with your tradition. Even a simple act, such as inviting participants to put their hands in a basin of water to remember their baptism, may be acceptable. If you are a layperson, talk with your pastor about how a brief service of remembrance could be enacted within this group.

Close the Session

Design a table for worship.

Set up a table where participants can see it. Prior to the session, gather a Bible, purple or multi-colored cloth, candles in assorted rainbow colors, a cross, a basin, and a pitcher of water.

Put the cloth on the table and explain either that purple is the color of penitence and so it is used during Lent or that the multi-colored cloth reminds us of God's rainbow covenant. Call on volunteers to come in turn to the table, select one of the elements you have gathered, and briefly state why it is included on this worship table.

Read Psalm 25 as a prayer.

Encourage participants to gather around the worship table. Read aloud Psalm 25:1-10, or if your hymnals include a Psalter, distribute them and invite the participants to read those verses responsively. Preface the reading by pointing out that the psalmist in some way feels as if he is drowning, for he seeks God's salvation and forgiveness even as he offers his life to God.

2. Trust and Obey

BIBLE BACKGROUND

What does it mean to live in covenant with God? This week's readings point to answers to that profound question. In the first reading from Genesis 17, God's covenant with Abraham is spelled out. To live in this covenantal relationship with God, the patriarch was to trust and obey, as the title for today's lesson observes. In Romans 4, Paul pointed to Abraham as the prime example of one who was put right with God by faith, which Abraham exhibited long before God gave the Law. The Gospel reading from Mark records Jesus' teachings, both in private to the disciples and in public to the crowd, about how one is to live in covenant with him by taking up the cross and following him.

Genesis 17:1-7, 15-16

Readers of Genesis first learned in Chapter 12 that God entered a special relationship with Abram, which would later be formalized in a covenant. At that time, Abram was seventy-five years old (12:4). Although recorded shortly after God's covenant with Noah, with all humanity, and with all creation following the Flood (9:8-17), the covenant with Abram is different in several ways. First, God made it with only one person, Abram. Second, God made specific promises to the patriarch: land, which would be the land of Canaan; descendants, who would become a great nation; and blessing, which would extend to Abram and through him to "all the families of earth" (12:3). In today's reading from Chapter 17, Abram was now ninety-nine years old (17:1). God called Abram to "walk" and "be trustworthy" (17:1), for God was about to make a covenant with him. Again, God promised the patriarch numerous descendants and the land of Canaan, as well as God's presence with them. This covenant necessitated a name change for both Abram and his wife, Sarai. He was to be called *Abraham*, meaning ancestor of a multitude, and she would be known as *Sarah*, which means princess. This was a fitting name for a woman whose offspring would include kings (17:16).

The accounts of God's covenant with Abraham in Chapter 17 and God's covenant with Noah and all life (Chapter 9) both come from authors that Bible scholars identify as "priestly" writers. These writers believed that each major period in history began with a covenant. Moreover, God is the one who "sets up" (17:7) or "establishes" (NRSV) an "enduring" (17:7) or "everlasting" (NRSV) covenant. Covenants include signs, such as the rainbow in Chapter 9 and circumcision in Chapter 17 (verses 10-11). Circumcision was to symbolize the blessings and descendants that God promised to Abraham and the generations that followed. The priestly writers were editing these stories during the period of the Babylonian exile. Readers even today can glimpse their faith, for in the midst of captivity and despair, their claim was that God's promises were still valid despite appearances to the contrary.

Romans 4:13-25

Writing to the church in Rome, which he had neither founded nor visited, the apostle Paul explained to the congregation how by grace through faith, believers are saved. In Romans 3:21–4:25 he discussed how God extends righteousness to sinners who receive this gift of salvation by faith. Paul began by describing how Jesus, through his death, made atonement for sinners. God counts among the righteous those who in faith believe. Then in 4:1-25 Paul cited Abraham, who he thought to be the best example of one who has authentic faith, to show that God has always considered faith—not works— the means by which people are reconciled to God.

God made the covenant promise to Abraham long before giving the Law to Moses on Mount Sinai. Since Abraham was put right with God before the Law existed, his justification could only be made through faith "on the basis of God's grace" (4:16). Paul emphasized Abraham's faith in verses 19-22. The elderly man and his wife Sarah were far past childbearing years, but Abraham was not swayed by circumstances. Instead, "he was fully convinced that God was able to do what he promised" (4:21). For that reason, God "credited [it] to him as righteousness" (4:22). Similarly, those who believe in the God who raised Jesus from the dead will also have that faith credited to them as righteousness (4:24).

Abraham had faith that God could fulfill a promise even in a seemingly hopeless situation. The eventual birth of Isaac to Sarah and Abraham showed their faith to be well placed. Likewise, as impossible as it seems that a human being could be raised from the dead, Christians believe that God raised Jesus Christ. During Lent, as believers look forward to the celebration of Jesus' resurrection on Easter, they recall and give thanks for the divine grace that made salvation possible for all who believe.

Mark 8:31-38

Prior to Mark 8:31, Jesus had called disciples, performed healings and exorcisms, told several parables, been rejected in his hometown of Nazareth, sent the Twelve out to minister, fed five thousand and later four thousand, walked on water, verbally sparred with the Pharisees, and heard Peter declare that Jesus was the Messiah. Today's reading from Mark 8:31-38 is especially appropriate for the season of Lent, because for the first of three times, Jesus foretold his death and resurrection. (The second time is in Mark 9:30-32 and the third, 10:32-34.) At 8:31, "Jesus began to teach." His students were first the disciples (8:31-33) and then the crowd (8:34-38). The content of his teaching concerns not only his future but also what will be required of those who make a commitment to follow him.

Jesus told his disciples that he would suffer, be rejected by the religious leaders, be killed, and rise from the dead. Peter, who had just declared Jesus as "the Christ" (the Messiah), scolded him. In turn, Jesus rebuked Peter because he was looking at the situation from the human perspective (verse 33). Peter could not imagine that God's Anointed One would be rejected, suffer, and die. By rebuking Jesus, Peter acted as if he knew better than Jesus. The disciple had tried to elevate himself to the position of teacher. Jesus, however, told Peter that his rejection of the path Jesus was to walk was tantamount to opposing him as Satan would.

Verse 34 makes clear that the suffering of the cross-formed life was not just for the Twelve but for all who choose to follow Jesus. They must deny themselves and take up their cross, which is to be understood in the context of proclaiming and living out the good news of Jesus. People have a choice about whether they want to risk their lives by following Jesus. But this choice has serious, far-reaching, eternal consequences. Apostasy will be reckoned with at the end of the age when the "Human One" (8:38), or "Son of Man" (NRSV), comes again in glory.

SESSION PLAN

Open the Session

Solicit a volunteer to read the introduction to this week's lesson.

Say: "Our writer recalls the trust required to go on a whitewater rafting trip to an unknown place with people who were unfamiliar to her. The newbie to this sport needs to learn to trust her fellow rafters and obey the guide who gives directions." Ask: What experiences have you had that similarly called you to trust and obey someone else?

Offer a prayer.

Lord of our salvation, you care so lovingly for each of us. May we respond to you with trust, obedience, and thanksgiving for all you have done for us. In Jesus' name we pray. Amen.

Engage the Scriptures

Explore a covenant.

Choose a volunteer to read Genesis 17:1-7, 15-16.

Form several teams, and assign one of the following questions to each. Suggest that participants use information under "Lords and Contracts," the Bible Background for Genesis 17, and their Bibles, to answer the question.

- Group 1: What did you learn about covenants in Abraham's day?
- Group 2: What are the features of the covenant between Abraham and God discussed in today's reading?
- Group 3: What difference did having a covenant with God make in the lives of Abraham, Sarah, and their descendants?

Call everyone together and ask a spokesperson for each group to summarize the responses to the group's assigned question.

Close by asking: God's covenant with Abraham and Sarah demonstrated God's evolving commitment to them. How does God's commitment to you make a difference in your life? How do you respond to this commitment?

Roleplay a covenant story.

Invite participants to read Genesis 17:1-7, 15-16 silently. Suggest that as they read, they try to put themselves in Abraham's sandals and let God's words of promise sink into their hearts and minds.

Read or summarize the Bible Background for Genesis. Emphasize that God first spoke to Abraham twenty-four years prior to this encounter (Genesis 12:4).

Call on several volunteers to do a roleplay between Abraham and Sarah in which he tells her what God has told him. Encourage each set of role players to dig deeper into the Bible story by asking questions of one another and sharing their feelings about what God is doing in their lives.

Investigate Paul's understanding of God's promise to Abraham.

Choose a reader for Romans 4:13-25.

Suggest that participants quickly review "Discovering Our Ancestors." Ask:

1. What points does Paul make to show that Abraham's promise came by faith, not by Law?
2. How did Abraham demonstrate his faith?
3. How do you understand that faith is "credited" as righteousness, not only to Abraham but also to you (4:23-24)?
4. How does your group or congregation demonstrate its faith?

Create a legacy of faith.

Form teams of three, and ask them to discuss this question: How do you want your descendants to remember you?

Reconvene and invite a volunteer to read Romans 4:13-25, and then ask: What legacy did Abraham and Sarah leave for their descendants? (Be sure to include their legacy of faith in God.)

Distribute paper and pencils. Encourage participants to write briefly about the kind of faith legacy they are leaving for their descendants (or other people who know them). Some participants may find it helpful to write their ideas as a letter to a particular person. Suggest that they write about how they have tried to live so that their faith can be seen and experienced by others. Recommend that they include those faith-filled actions, attitudes, and beliefs they yearn to convey to those they will leave behind.

Urge participants to review their papers throughout the week and do whatever is necessary to strengthen the legacy of faith they intend to leave.

Consider Jesus' directions for following him.

Distribute paper and pencils. Direct participants to jot down any instructions Jesus gave the crowd for following him as they listen to you read Mark 8:31-38.

Talk about the instructions that caught the participants' attention. Discuss what the instructions might mean in terms of how believers live their lives. Try to elicit concrete examples from the group. (For a summary, point out the paragraph beginning "The word 'must' occurs . . ." under "Crosses and Electric Chairs.")

Clarify what "taking up the cross" really means by looking at "Crosses and Electric Chairs," beginning with "Today, we wear . . ." through the words "life rather than restore it." Invite participants to give other examples of ways that individual believers and the church as a body can stand up in Jesus' name, despite the consequences.

Envision yourself with Jesus.

Invite participants to imagine themselves walking with Jesus by reading this brief script based on Mark 8:

You have come to hear Jesus teach. See yourself and four thousand other people eating a meal from just seven loaves of bread and a few fish, and then watching the disciples collect seven baskets of leftovers (8:1-10). What would you want to say to Jesus about this experience (pause)?

On another occasion, you bring a blind friend to Jesus at Bethsaida and he restores your friend's sight (8:22-26). What would you be thinking about who Jesus might be and why he would take time for you and your friend?

You are on your way to Caesarea Philippi when you overhear Peter testify that Jesus is the Christ, God's Anointed One, the Messiah (8:27-30). Based on everything you have seen and heard, who do you say that he is?

Now listen as Jesus teaches some remarkable things about what would happen to him—and to you. Read aloud Mark 8:31-38 and discuss these questions:

1. What would you have wanted to ask Jesus about verse 31?
2. What would you say to Peter privately after the group had dispersed?
3. After hearing Jesus' words in verses 36-38, what would you want to know about gaining and losing life?
4. What decision would you make about following Jesus? Why?

Close the Session

Read and reflect on Psalm 22.

Ask participants to read Psalm 22:1-22 silently. Point out that Psalm 22 is quoted or alluded to in the following New Testament passages, which are mainly from accounts of Jesus' crucifixion. Post this information:

22:1—Matthew 27:46; Mark 15:34
22:7—Matthew 27:39; Mark 15:29; Luke 23:35
22:8—Matthew 27:43
22:18—John 19:24; see also Matthew 27:35; Mark 15:24; Luke 23:34
22:22—Hebrews 2:12

Choose volunteers to read from the list above both the verse from Psalm 22 and each place in the New Testament where the psalm is quoted. After each set of verses is read, discuss how participants see Jesus' words in Mark 8 being foretold in Psalm 22 and fulfilled in the respective New Testament quotations.

Read aloud Psalm 22:23-31. Conclude by asking: How does Psalm 22 prompt you to trust and obey God as you pick up the cross?

Offer a prayer adapted from the hymn "Trust and Obey." [1]

Gracious Lord, as we walk with you in the light of your Word, help us willingly to lay all on the altar, knowing that as we trust and obey we will be happy and blessed in Jesus. Amen.

1. From *The United Methodist Hymnal* (Copyright © 1989 by The United Methodist Publishing House); 467.

3. Truth and Carnival Mirrors

BIBLE BACKGROUND

The readings from Exodus and John are connected by the Law that sets forth God's covenant. The first reading recounts God's giving of the Ten Commandments, which enable people to rightly relate with God and to live peaceably with one another. In John's Gospel, Jesus disrupted the system of animal sales and money exchange that had been established for worshippers to fulfill the law by purchasing a flawless animal for sacrifice. Jesus was furious that God's house had become a marketplace. In responding to the Jewish leaders, Jesus affirmed his authority and commented on his death and resurrection. In the Epistle reading, Paul differentiated between the world's wisdom and God's wisdom, which is rooted in the scandal of the cross on which Jesus died to bring salvation.

Exodus 20:1-17

The theme of covenant is again prominent this week. The Ten Commandments can be divided into two segments: The first four commandments concern the relationship of God's people to God; the second six focus on the relationship of God's people to one another.

According to verse 1, "God spoke all these words." There was no intermediary. The God who spoke—"your God"—was the same one who liberated the Hebrew people from slavery in Egypt (verse 2). These people were saved not because they had obeyed the Law, which had not previously been revealed to them, but because God took action to free them. As Christians would later assert, salvation came not on the basis of human action but because of God's gracious initiative.

The first three commandments not only draw boundaries for God's people but also disclose facets of God's nature. God is passionate and as such demands that people be loyal to this God alone. The Sovereign God cannot be contained in any "graven image" (20:4, KJV). Nor can God be manipulated or exploited by the wrongful use of God's name, according to the third commandment, which reflected the ancient belief that one who knew the name of a deity could appropriate divine power.

The fourth commandment, concerning the Sabbath, recalls God's work during the six days of creation and rest on the seventh. All people and their animals are also to rest. The Sabbath has status as a special day not because people are to worship then, but because they are to rest as God rested.

The remaining six commandments explain the rights and responsibilities willed by God for human life in community. People are to accord dignity to one another and treat one another with respect. Actions that abuse, exploit, or demean are not allowed within the community. These commandments form the foundation of life as God intends it to be lived.

1 Corinthians 1:18-25

During the season of Lent, believers focus attention on the cross. In writing to the church at Corinth, Paul also focused on the cross by contrasting its message with that of human wisdom. In verse 21, the apostle pointed out that one could not know God by means of human wisdom. Rather, the cross, though seen by those sinful ones who were dying as "foolishness," was actually the basis for salvation because it was "the power of God" (1:18).

As a well-educated Pharisaic Jew and Roman citizen, Paul understood the perspectives of both Jews and Greeks. He knew that the idea of a suffering Messiah was contrary to Jewish expectations. According to Deuteronomy 21:22-23, those "guilty of a capital crime" were to be hanged on a tree, and such criminals were cursed by God. How, then, could one crucified on a tree be the Messiah? The notion of "Christ crucified" was, therefore, "a scandal to the Jews" (1:23). The Greeks who heard preaching about Jesus also could not accept him, but for different reasons. They looked for "wisdom" (1:22), which was why philosophers were so revered among them. Greek mythology and literature is filled with noble heroes, not people who died shameful deaths. Jesus did not fit into the Greek ideal of a hero.

Paul drew a sharp line between the wisdom of the world and the wisdom of God. Those who were not being saved relied on the world's wisdom. But those who were being saved recognized Christ as being both "God's power and God's wisdom" (1:24). Moreover, there is no comparison between the wisdom of the world and the wisdom of God. Even what appears to be foolishness on the part of God is far wiser than what passes for the world's wisdom. People may try to make sense of what God is doing by using human wisdom as their measuring stick. But the reality is that God's wisdom cannot be discerned in this way.

John 2:13-22

Having returned to Capernaum after attending a wedding in Cana, Jesus went to Jerusalem to celebrate Passover. This was one of three festivals—Passover, Pentecost, and Booths (Tabernacles)—that Jewish males were expected to participate in at the Jerusalem Temple (see Exodus 23:14-17 and Deuteronomy 16:1-17). As an observant Jew, Jesus was among the many pilgrims in Jerusalem at this time.

Jesus arrived to find people "selling cattle, sheep, and doves" (2:14), which were sacrificial animals prescribed by law (Leviticus 1, 3). The animal had to be "flawless" (Leviticus 1:3, 10; 3:1, 6). Since worshippers, especially those who traveled from a distance, could not be certain that their sacrifices would be "flawless" by the time they reached the Temple, a system was in place that enabled them to purchase their sacrifices when they arrived. In order to buy their sacrifices, pilgrims first needed to convert their foreign currency to Temple currency. Jesus would have been familiar with this scene, because he had come to the Temple since childhood (Luke 2:41-51). As he began his public ministry, the values Jesus espoused concerning the sanctity of the Temple conflicted with the usual business practices there. He took action and chased the sellers as well as the animals out of the Temple area. Shocked by his boldness, the Temple leaders demanded to know who gave Jesus authority to take such action. They also asked for a sign, to which Jesus replied, "Destroy this temple and in three days I'll raise it up" (2:19). As is common in John's Gospel, Jesus' meaning was unclear to his listeners. They assumed he was talking about the Temple building, but he was referring to his bodily death and resurrection. After Jesus had been raised, the disciples remembered what he had said and as a result believed (2:22). The purpose of John's Gospel is to encourage people to "believe that Jesus is the Christ, God's Son" (20:31), so the disciples' belief fulfilled this goal.

Although all four Gospels include an account of Jesus cleansing the Temple, only John situates it at the beginning of Jesus' ministry. The others record this event shortly before his passion and death (see Matthew 21:12-13; Mark 11:15-19; Luke 19:45-46).

SESSION PLAN

Open the Session

Select a volunteer to read aloud the introduction to "Truth and Carnival Mirrors."

Encourage participants to talk about their own experiences with funhouse mirrors.

Ask these questions:

1. What distortions do you find in politics, business, culture, or your personal life? What about in the church?
2. How can these distortions be corrected?
3. What role might Jesus Christ play in making those corrections?

Offer a Prayer.

Gracious God, help us to see you more clearly so that we might recognize misleading views of the world and proclaim truth to all who will listen. Amen.

Engage the Scriptures

Delve into the Ten Commandments.

Choose ten volunteers to read the commandments as follows: Exodus 20:1-3; verses 4-6; verse 7; verses 8-11; verse 12; verse 13; verse 14; verse 15; verse 16; verse 17.

Form two teams (or multiple teams if the total group is large). Charge the first team with reading "Won't You Be My Neighbor?" to discern the people for whom the commandments were originally written, the distorted system that had governed their lives for generations, and how God expected these words to shape the lives of the covenant people as they moved forward into the Promised Land. Ask the second team to discern the purposes of these commandments by reading the Bible Background for Exodus 20:1-17.

Call everyone together and hear reports from each of the teams.

Ask: What new understandings did you gain from today's study about the purpose and meaning of the Ten Commandments?

Connect Psalm 19 to the Ten Commandments.

Invite participants to turn in their Bibles to Exodus 20:1-17 and scan these familiar commandments. Note that the first four commandments teach how people are to relate to God; the second six teach how people are to relate to one another as neighbors.

Point out that the themes or events of the Old Testament readings are frequently reflected in the lectionary psalm for the day. Consequently, the psalm is often read by the congregation as a response to the Old Testament lection.

Distribute hymnals if the ones you have access to include a Psalter. Form three teams, and ask each team to read a portion of Psalm 19 in unison: Team 1: verses 1-6; Team 2: verses 7-10; Team 3: verses 11-14. (If you have no Psalter available, choose three readers who have the same Bible translation to read the three sets of verses.) Discuss these questions:

1. How is God's glory seen in verses 1-6? (God as Creator)
2. How is God's glory seen in verses 7-10? (God as the giver of the Law)
3. What does the psalmist/servant ask of God in verses 11-14?
4. Some Christians erroneously put down the Law as burdensome. How are God's commandments perceived in this psalm?

5. What do you think the psalmist might say if he were asked how God's commandments correct the distortions of the world's way of treating others and open people's eyes to truth?

Contrast human wisdom with God's wisdom.

Choose a volunteer to read the Epistle lesson from 1 Corinthians 1:18-25. Post a large sheet of paper. On the top left write "Human Wisdom" and on the top right write "God's Wisdom." Encourage participants to look at their Bibles to find descriptive words or phrases for each side of the paper.

Add to what has been written by suggesting that participants scan "The Wisdom of Fools" and call out additional descriptive words or phrases. Ask:

1. How does society encourage you to rely on human wisdom?
2. What struggles have you faced in trying to be loyal to Christ and his cross when others told you that was "foolishness"?
3. How are you and your church helping others to see that following Christ is the wisest way to live?
4. What steps can your congregation (or denomination) take to make clearer that reliance on God's wisdom is the way to correct the distortions that society claims as truth?

Summarize a Bible teaching from First Corinthians.

Form several small teams. If possible, have at least two Bible translations per team. Ask the teams to read 1 Corinthians 1:18-25, followed by "The Wisdom of Fools." Several Bible commentaries would also be helpful.

Distribute a large sheet of paper and marker to each team, and ask them to write one or two sentences that sum up the core of Paul's teaching in this passage. Give each team an opportunity to read aloud their summary. Evaluate the areas in which teams agreed and disagreed with one another.

Conclude the activity, if time permits, by writing a single summary that all of the teams can agree on.

Pantomime a Bible story from John.

Tell participants to read silently John 2:13-22. Select several people to pantomime this story—that is, act it out without using words. One person will act as Jesus; four or five will act as the moneychangers Jesus drove out of the Temple; two or three others will act as the Jewish leaders; the rest of the participants will watch as the disciples did. (Adjust the number of players if you have fewer than eight total participants.) Read the passage yourself, allowing enough time for the actors to respond. Debrief the pantomime by asking:

1. The system of sacrifices and currency exchange had existed in the Temple for many years. What prompted Jesus to respond the way he did?
2. What is the misunderstanding between what Jesus said and what the Jewish leaders thought he was referring to?
3. How did this incident enable the disciples to believe in Jesus?
4. Had you been a worshipper standing in line to exchange your money or buy your sacrifice, how would Jesus' words and actions have affected you?

Identify tables the church needs to overturn.

Choose someone to read John 2:13-22. Direct participants' attention to "Turning Tables," and ask someone to read from "I am an institutional girl" through "ritual and rules." Point out that our writer has suggested "tables" that she would like to see overturned from her perspective as an ordained pastor.

Distribute paper (preferably unlined) and pencils. Direct participants to tear their sheets into three equal pieces. On each piece, participants are to write one "table" that they would like to see overturned because they believe it has distorted God's will for the church. Collect the papers. Tack or tape them to a wall or large sheet of paper for all to see. Notice duplicate responses. Ask:

1. What might we do as a group to begin to overturn these tables?
2. Which table would we as a group want to overturn first?

Close the Session

Release distortions.

Bring at least one handheld mirror. Pass around the mirror(s) as you ask participants to look at their reflections and think silently on these questions:

1. As I look in the mirror, what distortions can I identify in my own life?
2. Have I accepted as truth a belief that my culture insists upon, such as the need for status, power, and money? What can I do to release these distortions from my life?

Offer a prayer.

Gracious God, in the midst of all the distorted values and beliefs of the world, help us to know and live by your truth. In Jesus' name we pray. Amen.

4. Either/Or

BIBLE BACKGROUND

Today's readings present two opposite themes: judgment and grace. In Numbers, God sent deadly snakes to punish the people who constantly complained in the wilderness. In response to their pleas, God instructed Moses to construct a bronze snake on a pole. Those who were bitten could look at this gracious gift from God and be healed. Summoning the image of the bronze snake, Jesus explained in John 3 that he, too, would be "lifted up." His crucifixion would provide the gracious means of salvation for those who believed. Jesus would not judge those who did not believe in him, but by their own choice, they would live in darkness. The Epistle reading from Ephesians emphasizes the point that humans were "headed for punishment" (2:3) because of their disobedience. God graciously offered the gift of salvation through Jesus to those who accepted it by faith.

Numbers 21:4-9

This story is set in the wilderness as the Hebrews who had been liberated from Egypt continued their trek. With God's help, they had defeated the Canaanite king of Arad (Numbers 21:1-3). But soon they grew impatient and were again complaining about the food and water. To hear them tell the story, Egypt must have been a wonderful place! (See the first complaint story in Numbers 11.) That, of course, was not true. Although God faithfully provided manna for them, they declared "we detest this miserable bread!" (21:5). The people railed against both God and Moses. In response to this complaint, the Lord sent snakes whose venom was so poisonous that those who were bitten died. These snakes were described as "poisonous" or "fiery," which comes from a Hebrew verb that means to burn. According to verse 7, the people recognized their sin against both God and Moses and implored their leader to pray that God would "send the snakes away from us." Moses prayed for the people, but God did not answer the prayer in the way they had hoped. God instructed Moses to construct a bronze snake and set it on a pole. Anyone who was bitten could look at the pole and live. Thus, God did not take away the punishment of snakes slithering among the people, but rather provided a way to heal them if they would obey and look at the pole.

Even such a gracious gift from God could be exploited and turned into an idol. Second Kings 18:3-4 reports that the new king Hezekiah "did what was right in the LORD's eyes" by destroying improper shrines. Among the devotional objects he had crushed was the bronze snake, because the people "had been burning incense to it" (2 Kings 18:4). Although this object was created as a symbol of healing, by the time of Hezekiah (715 to circa 687 B.C.), it had become an idol, worshipped for its healing power.

Ephesians 2:1-10

The Letter to the church at Ephesus, traditionally ascribed to Paul, focuses on God's plan to reconcile Jews and Gentiles, even the entire universe, by means of the death and resurrection of Jesus. In today's reading, Paul described what life was like when people offended and became alienated from God. They were, to use Paul's term, "dead" because they "used to live like people of this world" (2:1-2). Such people did it their way, doing whatever felt good to them, rather than obeying God. Their behavior put them on a path hurtling toward punishment.

The believers to whom Paul was writing, however, were no longer dead. God had graciously saved them (2:5, 8). The Greek verb tense used for the word *saved* in these two verses indicates that the action of salvation that occurred in the past is ongoing. Verse 7 explains why God acted to save people: "to show future generations" God's goodness and grace, which is unmerited favor given by God in Christ. As a result of God's gracious mercy and love, they and all believers are "brought . . . to life with Christ" (2:4), "raised . . . up" (2:6), and "seated . . . with Christ" in heaven (2:6). The same God who created humanity initiated this remarkable change in human status (2:10). God gives salvation as a gift; it cannot be earned by anything that one does. Believers can only receive salvation through faith. As verse 8 reads: "You are saved by God's grace *because of your faith*" (emphasis added). An alternative reading of verse 8 says that people are saved "*through his faithfulness*" (emphasis added), thereby putting the onus of faith on Jesus himself.

The gift of salvation is offered to all, but as the title of today's lesson suggests, people need to choose: Either they will turn to Christ and receive the salvation that our loving God so freely offers, or they will continue following the ways of the world and "the rule of a destructive spiritual power" (2:2).

John 3:14-21

These verses follow the story of the conversation between Nicodemus and Jesus about how one can enter the kingdom of God. In verse 14, Jesus referred to the story from Numbers 21 of the bronze serpent being lifted up on a pole to bring healing to those in the wilderness who had been bitten by deadly snakes. He compared Moses' lifting up of this snake in the wilderness to his own "lifting up" that was to come. The image can be interpreted in two ways: Jesus would die by being raised up on the cross, but he would also be lifted up in glory through his death, resurrection, and ascension. Just as everyone who saw the snake was healed, likewise everyone who looks to the crucified and resurrected Christ will be saved from death. Jesus promised that believers would not die but would have eternal life. According to *The New Interpreter's Study Bible,* " 'eternal life' does not speak of immortality or a future life in heaven, but is a metaphor for living now in the unending presence of God."[1]

In verses 16-21, Jesus reflected on the meaning of his incarnation and life in this world. His purpose in coming was to bring salvation, not judgment. But salvation is dependent upon belief in him. The point here is that people condemn themselves when they refuse to believe in "God's only Son" (3:18). Jesus went on to explain the basis for judgment using two images often found in John's Gospel: light and darkness. To live in the revealing light of the incarnate Christ brings life (see John 1:4). This light "shines in the darkness" (1:5), thereby exposing whatever is evil.

SESSION PLAN

Open the Session

Review with participants the introduction to the session for the Fourth Sunday in Lent, titled "Either/Or." Distribute paper and pencils. Tell participants that you will quickly read a list of words. After each word is read, they are to write down a word that they think of as an opposite. In some cases, multiple answers may be possible. Read this list of words, adding others as you see fit: *dog, car, day, floor, boy, weed, hamburger, happy, old, generous.*

Mention that people often think in terms of either this or that. Sometimes one answer is as good as another, and then personal preference plays a role. In other cases, there is a marked difference between the two choices. Invite participants to consider the various sets of choices present in today's Scripture passages.

Offer a prayer.

God of Judgment and God of Grace, we give thanks that you created us with the free will to choose among competing options. Help us to make those choices that will enable us to live peaceably in your realm both now and eternally. Amen.

Engage the Scriptures

Encounter judgment and grace in the desert.

Introduce the reading from Numbers by reading or summarizing the Bible Background information for the Old Testament lection.

Call on a volunteer to read Numbers 21:4-9, and discuss these questions:

1. What choices do you think the Israelites had, both before they left Egypt and after they were in the wilderness?
2. Once God had declared judgment by sending snakes, what choice did the people have to experience God's grace?
3. Why do you think they held tightly to the past rather than open themselves to the future God had for them?
4. What prevents people today from leaping by faith into the future that God wants for them?

Weigh choices.

Choose a volunteer to read the first two and final two paragraphs in "Change or Die." Call on another volunteer to read Numbers 21:4-9.

Note that the choices the Kodak company had to make were in many ways similar to the choices the liberated Hebrews had to make while they were in the wilderness. Kodak and the Hebrews both clung to the past, even though a better future awaited them.

Post a large sheet of paper, and encourage participants to call out words or phrases to describe choices that they believe their congregation or denomination needs to make in order to continue to make disciples for Jesus Christ. List ideas on paper, but do not go into any details here. These choices could include adding a different kind of service or holding to the status quo; hiring or not hiring a youth director; starting a new ministry for a group not currently being served or reaching out in another way; and so forth.

Select three ideas, and form teams to consider the pros and cons of each.

Bring everyone back together. Encourage each team to state the choice that they feel is best and give their reasons. (Consider passing these ideas along to the appropriate staff and volunteers within the church.)

Do a Bible study.

Enlist three volunteers to read respectively Ephesians 2:1-3, 4-7, 8-10.

Form small teams. Encourage participants to review the Bible Background for Ephesians, and then discuss these questions, which you may wish to post on a large sheet of paper for easy reference:

1. What does this passage tell you about people who do not walk with God?
2. What does this passage tell you about how and why God acts on behalf of humanity?
3. What relationship do you see in this passage between God and humanity?

Reconvene and invite participants to echo these words from verse 5: "You are saved by God's grace!" Let these words remind participants that "salvation is God's gift" and not something they "possessed" (2:8).

Plan to help others choose life.

Choose a volunteer to read Ephesians 2:1-10 and ask:

1. Ephesians speaks in general terms about negative actions that lead to death: "wrong," "offenses against God," "destructive spiritual power," "spirit of disobedience," "do whatever felt good," "headed for punishment" (2:1-3). What specific actions might the author or audience have had in mind as they heard these general statements?
2. What specific actions in our own society indicate that a person has chosen death?
3. According to verses 4-10, what provisions has God made for people to choose life?

Select someone to read "Life or Death" beginning with "While I was in seminary . . ." and ending with "buy and sell women." Discuss the Magdalene program, which offers women a new start after prostitution and addiction.

Encourage participants to talk about other programs, including those in your church or community, that also offer people a path from death to life. List the names of these ministries on a large sheet of paper. Suggest that participants choose one or two programs of interest to them and contact the church or agency in charge to find out how they can go about volunteering to assist.

Use Lectio Divina to encounter John 3.

Say: "*Lectio Divina* is an ancient method of devotionally engaging the Scriptures. Although there are different ways to practice this method, four steps are fundamental: READ; REFLECT; RESPOND (to God); and REST (let go of our ideas and listen for God).[2] Instead of looking for the history and theology of the text, *Lectio Divina* invites an individual or group to let God's voice lead in pointing out important words and phrases to help readers on their spiritual journeys."

Invite the group to observe a time of silence, during which each participant will read John 3:14-21 quietly and slowly. You may wish to begin this period with a brief centering prayer. As they read, participants should reflect on a word or image in the text that seems to stand out to them. Next, they are to respond silently to God with their own thoughts, words, ideas, and so forth, as they would in a dialogue. Finally, they are to let go of these ideas and simply listen for God. Allow several minutes of silence for the group to try this method. Some members may return to read the biblical text over and over; others may not read all of the verses as they reflect and respond to a single word or phrase. Either of these is okay, since *Lectio Divina* is a set of guidelines for praying with the Scriptures rather than a rigid set of rules.

Call time, and invite volunteers to report on new insights, as well as how this method worked for them. Suggest that they use this method at home, taking whatever time feels right to them.

Set John 3:14-21 in context.

Choose someone to read the section on John 3:14-21 from the Bible Background. Read aloud John 3:14-21.

Recommend that participants scan the section titled "Up or Down."

Ask: How do the stories from Numbers 21:4-9 and John 3:1-10 help you to understand Jesus' message in John 3:14-21?

Close the Session

Vote up or down.

Read "Up or Down," from "For us, it all boils . . ." through the end of the paragraph. Direct everyone to close their eyes and answer this question with a "thumbs up" or "thumbs down" that only God will see: I accept the salvation that God sent Jesus into the world to offer and will live faithfully as one who believes in Jesus. Close by asking the group to recite John 3:16 with you.

Offer Psalm 107 as a closing prayer.

Note that in this hymn, the psalmist called people to give thanks for God's goodness and deliverance from adversity. Enlist four volunteers to read 107:1; verses 2-3; verses 17-18; and verses 19-20, with everyone reading verses 21-22 in unison from whatever Bible translations they have.

1. From *The New Interpreter's Study Bible*, page 1912, Special Note on eternal life.
2. See *http://ocarm.org/en/content/lectio/what-lectio-divina*.

5. Outcasts and Outsiders

BIBLE BACKGROUND

Suffering plays a pivotal role in this week's readings. The people of Jeremiah's time are "outcasts and outsiders" who have been wrested from the Promised Land and taken to Babylon to live as captives. Where was God in this horrific situation? Jeremiah's prophecy looked ahead to a time of restoration and renewal when the people would once again be in a close, personal relationship with God. Written to people who were suffering persecution for their faith, the Letter to the Hebrews points out that Jesus, our high priest, has been made perfect through suffering. As a result, he can be the source of our salvation. John's Gospel homes in on Jesus as the hour of both his suffering and glorification has come. He did not shirk from the cross but embraced it as the reason for which he became enfleshed and dwelled among humanity.

Jeremiah 31:31-34

Much of the Book of Jeremiah sounds a somber note during the turmoil of the Babylonian invasions that resulted in the collapse of Jerusalem and the exile of God's people. The first twenty-five chapters, which detail why the nation fell, are filled with accusations. In Chapter 26 through the end of the book, the prophet considered the aftermath of the fall and how the exiles might survive as a people, especially since they questioned whether God was still with them. Today's reading comes from a portion of Jeremiah, known as "the little book of consolation," that rings with hope.[1] The purpose of this section of the book is to provide glimpses of the future—to look ahead to a time when the people now living as captive exiles will live together in a renewed relationship with God. The wording suggests that the intimate familial relationship God once had with the people, described as a parent leading a child by the hand and as a husband (31:32), will be restored.

Jeremiah 31:31-34 is familiar to Christians. It speaks of a "new covenant" that was made with the people of Israel and Judah (31:31). Those to whom Jeremiah was writing and to whom God was speaking were the descendants of the slaves God had led out of Egypt, the ones who had broken God's covenant made through Moses. Unlike the Mosaic covenant that was written on two stone tablets, this "new covenant" would be "engraved" on the hearts of the people. *Heart* was understood by Jeremiah's audience to refer to the seat of one's will.

All of the covenant people will know God equally. Whether one is among the least or the greatest, the entire community will know God (31:34). This final verse ends with two remarkable promises: God will not only forgive the people for their sins but God will also "never again remember their sins."

Hebrews 5:5-10

Although it is often titled "The Letter to the Hebrews," scholars generally agree that this book is not a letter per se but rather a sermon that was sent as a letter. Traditionally ascribed to Paul, as early as the third century his authorship was called into question, though there are enough similarities to suggest that someone within Paul's circle may have been the writer.[2] Although the exact recipients of this document are unknown, it is clear that they had suffered persecution, perhaps under the Emperor Claudius in A.D. 49. Despite the fact that the author of Hebrews argued that the new covenant in Christ was superior to the former covenant, biblical commentator Donald A. Hagner points out "the discontinuity the author sees between old and new is contained within a larger continuity that sees the new as the proper outgrowth and fulfillment of the old."[3] Consequently, Christian readers need to tread carefully so as not to view this text from an anti-Semitic perspective that was never intended.

Today's reading continues a discussion that began in 4:14 concerning Jesus as the Great High Priest. Hebrews 5:1-4 explains how a high priest was chosen and the tasks he was to perform. Verse 5 connects the dots between Jesus and the office of the high priest in the Temple. Just as the high priest was "called by God" (5:4), so Jesus was "appointed" to this position by God (5:5-6, 10). Whereas the high priest was descended from Aaron, Jesus was the Son of God. He was a priest after the unique order of Melchizedek, the one to whom Abraham gave tithes and who blessed the patriarch long before the levitical priesthood established through Aaron existed (Genesis 14:17-20; see also Hebrews 7).

Appropriately, during this season of Lent, our reading from Hebrews highlights Jesus' suffering (5:7-8). His humanity is on display in these verses, for like the human high priests Jesus was tempted and can empathize with human weakness (4:15). Through suffering, he had been perfected and could therefore become "the source of eternal salvation for everyone who obeys him" (5:9).

John 12:20-33

After entering Jerusalem (12:12-19), Jesus began to speak about his impending death. He was quite aware that "the time has come" for him to be "glorified" (12:23). In John's Gospel, glorification refers to the death, resurrection, and exaltation of Jesus. He had made recent reference to his death in verse 7 after Judas groused about the waste of money on expensive perfume that Mary had used to anoint Jesus' feet (12:4-6). To counter Judas's criticism, Jesus had said that this perfume "was to be used in preparation for my burial, and this is how she has used it" (12:7). Mary had performed this loving act for Jesus, who had brought her brother Lazarus back from the dead. As a result of the people's positive response to Lazarus' reanimation, the Jewish leaders "plotted to kill" Jesus (11:53).

In John's Gospel, Jesus is portrayed as being in charge of events. He faced death head-on. He used the image of a seed to explain that his death would not be the end but rather a new beginning: Fruit is born when a single seed dies (12:24). Jesus was giving his life for the community of faith. In turn, those who followed him were also called to serve (12:26). In John, Jesus did not ask to be saved, because it was for this very hour that he had come (12:27). He called out to God to "glorify your name!" (12:28). God replied to Jesus, though the crowd was uncertain as to whether they had heard thunder or the voice of an angel. Whatever they had heard, Jesus made clear that the voice was for their benefit. Judgment was at hand, because Jesus' death marked the defeat of evil ("this world's ruler" in verse 31).

SESSION PLAN

Open the Session

Encourage participants to review the introduction for "Outcasts and Outsiders."

Post a large sheet of paper. Give each participant either an index card or a small sheet of paper and a marker or pencil. Tell participants to imagine their cards as bricks and write a situation or personal attribute that may make people feel as if they are "walled out" of the church. As participants finish, direct them to affix their cards to the large sheet of paper, using tape or tacks. The cards should be aligned in such a way that the paper resembles a brick wall.

Invite the group to ponder these situations and attributes for a few moments to identify any that have made them feel like outsiders.

Conclude by reading aloud the final paragraph in the introduction to remind the group that God's love is inclusive.

Offer a prayer.

Embracing God, help us to welcome all people just as you, through Jesus, have welcomed us. Let your love shine through us so that others may come into a saving relationship with your beloved Son. Amen.

Engage the Scriptures

Hear a new covenant.

Choose an expressive reader for Jeremiah 31:31-34. Suggest that participants imagine themselves as people who have witnessed the destruction of their city and way of life and who now wonder where God is. Participants are to listen for words or phrases that speak to them. Discuss these questions:

1. What is God promising to do?
2. How will this covenant differ from the one that God made at the time of the Exodus?
3. How do you feel hearing that God will forgive and forget your sins even though you and your ancestors have shattered your relationship with God?
4. What difference does it make to you that God will engrave the Law (instructions for living) on your heart so that you will know God in a more intimate way?

Help participants understand the initial purpose of this covenant by reading or paraphrasing the Bible Background for Jeremiah. Be sure they recognize that this was God's covenant with the Jews long before Christians read it as God's covenant with them through Jesus.

Seek forgiveness and transformation.

Recruit a reader for Jeremiah 31:31-34.

Select a volunteer to read "Failures" from "The new covenant God promises . . ." to the end of the section. Provide a time for quiet reflection by asking: Where does your heart need to break open so that it can be transformed?

End the silent time by leading the group in a reading of Psalm 51:1-12 as a cry for God to forgive their sins and cleanse them, just as David had asked of God after his sin with Bathsheba. If possible, read responsively from the Psalter in your hymnals. Otherwise, choose several readers who have the same Bible translation to read responsively, verse by verse.

Discern the meaning of Hebrews 5:5-10.

Form several small teams to read Hebrews 5:5-10, the Bible Background for Hebrews, and "Dirty" in the student section of the book.

Post these questions and assign one or two of them to each team:

1. What comparisons can you draw between the hidden dirtiness that our writer found in her home and what God sees in our hearts?
2. In what ways is Jesus the "housekeeper par excellence" of our body, mind, and spirit?
3. How would you describe the job of a priest and the personal attributes needed to do this job effectively?
4. How is Jesus similar to and different from the priests who are descended from Aaron?

Reconvene and call upon a spokesperson from each team to answer their assigned question(s). Invite anyone who wishes to add other insights gleaned from the discussion.

Research Melchizedek.

Call on a volunteer to read Hebrews 5:5-10. Note that the last verse mentions "the order of Melchizedek," a priest about whom little is known but who is referred to several times.

Provide at least one Bible dictionary and any other resources that discuss Melchizedek. Post on a large sheet of paper the following biblical references to Melchizedek: Genesis 14:17-20; Psalm 110:4; Hebrews 6:17–7:3; Hebrews 7:4-17. Depending on the size of the group, work in pairs or small teams to research this elusive priest and determine why Jesus was said to be a priest of his order. Call on volunteers to report their findings about Melchizedek.

Enact Jesus' teaching.

Select five volunteers to read the parts of a storyteller, two Greeks, Jesus, and a voice from heaven in John 12:20-33. Ask several participants to read the crowd's words in verse 29 and the remainder of the group to read what the "others" said in verse 29. Allow a few moments for each person to review silently his or her assigned parts, and then read aloud.

Embed this scene in participants' memories by planting seeds of some easy-to-grow vegetables or flowers. (The seeds you choose will vary by your location.) Also, have small paper cups, potting soil, a table, and covering for the table. Participants are to plant a single seed in each cup and take it home to nurture it, perhaps planting it outdoors when the time is right. Remind participants that although each of these seeds has died, Jesus reminded his disciples that a seed can bear much fruit by dying in this way.

Form a cohesive team.

Select someone to read "Welcome." Note especially the paragraphs beginning with "In the 2014 Sochi Winter Olympics . . ." and ending with "dashed as well."

Form two teams and give each a large sheet of paper and a marker. One team is to discuss and list actions and attitudes that make for a cohesive team. The other team is to discuss and list actions and attitudes that prevent a team from becoming unified. Provide time for each team to present its ideas.

Link these ideas to today's Gospel lesson by enlisting someone to read John 12:20-33. Then discuss these questions:

1. How can a congregation (or denomination) work to avoid divisive actions and attitudes to focus on building a cohesive team of believers?
2. What changes need to occur so that our actions and attitudes respect diversity while building unity?
3. What first steps can we take—or encourage the church to take—to create more solidarity within the congregation?

Close the Session

Practice hospitality.

Recall that today's stories are connected by the theme of people suffering because they were outsiders and outcasts. They yearned for welcome where their differences would no longer be a stumbling block.

Ask: What are some ways that we can welcome others into worship, educational groups, or mission opportunities? List these ideas on a large sheet of paper.

Distribute paper and pencils. Challenge participants to write the name(s) of anyone they could invite to attend these Lenten sessions and/or worship with them. Encourage the group to be prepared to welcome all who come.

Offer a prayer.

Gracious Lord, through Jesus you have welcomed each of us into your household. Show us how we can open our hearts to welcome others into your realm. In Jesus' name we pray. Amen.

1. From *The New Interpreter's Study Bible*, page 1100, footnote for 30:1–33:26.

2. From *The New Interpreter's Study Bible*, page 2151-2152.

3. From *The New Interpreter's Study Bible*, page 2152.

6. Justice

BIBLE BACKGROUND

What constitutes justice in God's realm? Is the physical abuse of God's servant just? Is the emptying of self and taking on human flesh just? Is the Crucifixion of the One who came to serve and save humanity just? According to human definitions, each of these situations represents a gross miscarriage of justice. Yet each of these demonstrates just how far God was willing to go to reconcile humanity to God's own self. The theme of suffering, which comes to the forefront as Holy Week begins, is intertwined with God's way of bringing about justice. Humans have indeed sinned, but God's Son voluntarily poured himself out so that those who believe might be justified—made right—with God.

Isaiah 50:4-9a

Scholars have identified four "servant songs" within the book of Isaiah. The one for today's study is the third song; the other three are found in 42:1-4; 49:1-6; and 52:13–53:12. These songs were written while Israel was in exile, likely near the end of their sojourn in Babylon. These prophetic messages of salvation were truly good news for those Judeans who, along with their descendants, had been held captive for half a century. Freedom was coming, but so was more suffering, which is why this song is so appropriate for the Sixth Sunday in Lent, known as Palm/Passion Sunday.

The third song begins in verses 4-5a with a biographical note in which the servant explained his relationship to God and his vocation. The words *tongue, word, ear,* and *listen* point to the servant's vocation as a communicator and teacher. The people he was to teach and converse with were those "weary" exiles (50:4). This vocation was not for the faint of heart, for the servant endured physical abuse. He did not fight back but relied on God to help him and "vindicate" him (50:8, NRSV). He challenged anyone who wanted to "bring judgment" against him to "stand up together" with him (50:8) as in a court of law. The servant knew that with God on his side no one would be able to condemn him.

The unidentified "servant" in Isaiah could refer to the prophet himself, or perhaps to all of Israel. However, the early church saw Jesus fulfilling the role of servant. Although he suffered as a result of his vocation, he knew that his words were God's words and that God would prove him correct in the end.

Philippians 2:5-11

In this part of Philippians, Paul has likely quoted a hymn known in the early church. This hymn, found in verses 6-11, can be diagrammed as the letter V. The left side illustrates the descent of Christ to humanity (2:6-8); the right side, his exaltation (2:9-11). Beginning in the upper left hand corner, the preexistent Christ who was "in the form of God" then "emptied himself." He voluntarily gave up the equality he had with God to take the form of a human—specifically, a slave. He was willing humbly to obey God even though that obedience led him to death on a cross, which is represented as the bottom of the V. These themes of suffering and death, seen on the left side of the V, strike at the deepest meaning of Palm/Passion Sunday.

The word "therefore" in verse 9 signals a transition from one "actor" to another: Jesus was no longer the one orchestrating the action; God took charge, "highly honored" Jesus (2:9), and named him "Lord." Christ was the one who emptied himself, took the form of a slave, humbled himself, and became obedient. But it was God who exalted him by raising Jesus from the dead and empowering him to ascend into heaven. As a result of the humbling actions of Jesus and exalting actions of God, all people and all creation can confess Jesus the Christ as Lord (2:11).

This hymn is linked to Paul's exhortation in verse 5: The saving activity of Christ, narrated in the hymn of verses 6-11, forms the basis for the believers' Christlike attitudes here and now.

Mark 15:1-39 (40-47)

Jesus was arrested (14:43-52) and taken before the Jewish council (14:53-65) where he was accused of blasphemy (14:64). Since Jewish law called for the execution of a blasphemer by means of stoning (Leviticus 24:16), the Sanhedrin "formed a plan" (15:1). They would turn Jesus over to Pontius Pilate, the governor of Judea from A.D. 26-36 who answered to the emperor Tiberius Caesar. Pilate's question in verse 2—"Are you the king of the Jews?"—suggests that the Jewish leaders told Pilate he should be charged with insurrection. Mark's portrait of Pilate, particularly in verse 10, made him appear sympathetic to Jesus, who he apparently considered innocent. Historical accounts of Pilate's ruthless behavior indicate, however, that he would not have hesitated to find a charged person guilty. Jesus did not answer the charge and for that reason alone, according to some historians familiar with Roman legal proceedings, he would have been found guilty.[1]

As Mark 15 continues, Pilate handed Jesus over for crucifixion, which was a brutal form of capital punishment used mainly in cases involving slaves, robbers, and those inciting insurrection. According to custom, Pilate would release one prisoner at Passover (15:6). Whipped up by the Jewish leadership (15:11), the crowd called for the release of Barabbas, who had been imprisoned for committing murder during a rebel uprising (15:7). Ironically, by agreeing to the crowd's demands, Pilate freed Barabbas, who was guilty of insurrection, and crucified the innocent Jesus.

Roman soldiers mocked Jesus by dressing him in the purple robe of royalty, putting a crown of thorns on his head, and addressing him as "King of the Jews" before leading him to Golgotha (15:16-22). The actual Crucifixion is described in sparse detail, but for the fifth time in Mark 15, Jesus is referred to as "the king of the Jews" (15:26). Although derision was intended, without meaning to do so, Pilate and the soldiers spoke truth about who Jesus was as a descendant of King David. In verse 39, a Roman soldier referred to Jesus not as king, but as "God's Son." The chapter concludes with an account of the burial of Jesus.

SESSION PLAN

Open the Session

Read the introduction to this week's Bible Background.

Solicit a volunteer to read Psalm 31:9-16 and then ask: Where do you see glimpses of Jesus' suffering during Holy Week in this psalm?

Allow a few minutes for silent reflection on this question: How might these verses describe your own life? What grief, sadness, or suffering currently plagues you?

End the silent time by reading aloud the final paragraph of the introduction for today's session, "Justice."

Offer a prayer.

Make your comforting presence known in our suffering, Precious Lord, even as you endured the suffering on the cross of your Son, in whose name we pray. Amen.

Engage the Scriptures

Relate to an anecdote.

Choose someone to read "Bug Bites," beginning with "I have never . . ." and ending with "stand there and take it."

Ask participants to talk with a partner about a time when they had to "stand there and take it."

Bring everyone together and have a volunteer read the third servant song from Isaiah 50:4-9a.

Invite someone else to read from "Bug Bites," beginning with the words "In these verses . . ." through "because of that hope;" then skip to "In the midst of trials and tribulations . . ." and read to the end of the section.

Conclude by asking: How do the experiences of the bug-bitten preacher and the suffering servant help you to recognize and lean on God's promises, even when you feel like you cannot take it anymore?

Survey Isaiah's servant songs.

Read or summarize information from the Bible Background about Isaiah.

Form four teams and assign each team to one of Isaiah's songs: Isaiah 42:1-4; 49:1-6; 50:4-9a; 52:13–53:12. Note that the song in Chapter 50 is today's reading. Be sure that each team has at least one Bible so that they can read their assigned passage. Each team will answer all of these questions:

1. What does God expect the Servant to do?
2. How is the Servant's work expected to bring about justice?
3. What evidence of suffering do you see in your passage?

Reconvene the teams. Post three sheets of large paper. Ask the first question, and record each team's response to each question on the sheet.

Ask: Although the Servant was never specifically identified, the early church saw Jesus in these four servant songs. Where do you see Jesus in these songs?

Diagram the structure of a Bible song.

Draw a V on a large sheet of paper. Call on two volunteers, one to read Philippians 2:6-8 and the other to read verses 9-11. Encourage the listeners to follow this early song of the church as it begins in the upper left hand corner, slides down to the bottom of the V and moves up the right side. Ask the following questions. Use information from the Bible Background for the Philippians passage to enrich the discussion.

1. How would you describe Jesus on the left side of the V?
2. How would you describe Jesus on the right side of the V?
3. What did he do—and what did God do—to change Jesus' status?

Envision Jesus as an underdog.

Select a volunteer to read Philippians 2:5-11. As an alternative, if you have access to *The United Methodist Hymnal*, responsively read an adaptation of these verses found in number 167.

Point out that although we generally focus on the power and majesty of Jesus as seen in verses 9-11, during this Holy Week, we can also see him as an underdog in verses 6-8. Suggest that participants review the section titled "Underdogs" to be prepared to discuss these questions:

1. Poet and playwright Jessica Hagedorn defined *underdogs* as persons "who seem to be not considered valuable in polite society." As you think about Philippians 2:6-8, what evidence do you see that Jesus could have been labeled an underdog?
2. What kinds of people are underdogs in our society, people who are not considered valuable and likely suffer from oppression and injustice?
3. God exalted Jesus and in doing so raised him from underdog status. What can the church do to help those who live as underdogs to find dignity and justice?

Chart Jesus' last hours.

Note that today's Gospel lection begins with Jesus' trial before Pilate and ends with his burial. Form six teams, and give each one a large sheet of paper and a marker. Assign passages to the teams: Mark 15:1-5; verses 6-15; verses 16-20; verses 21-32; verses 33-41; verses 42-47. Direct each team to create a chart as follows and fill in information based on their assigned Bible passage: Who was around Jesus? What was happening? When did the action take place (verses and time)? Where was Jesus? Why did the event(s) occur?

Direct the teams to mount their charts on a wall in chronological order. Invite one person from each team to tell the story of what was happening.

Conclude by discussing these two questions with the total group:

1. Had you been one of Jesus' female followers (15:40-41), what would you want to say or do to those who were crucifying Jesus?
2. As a Christian who believes that Jesus died for you, what emotions run through your mind as you read this very familiar story?

Probe feelings.

Ask: Under what circumstances have you felt helpless?

Select a volunteer to read "Helpless," starting with the words "In the fall . . ." and ending with "powerless to help."

Note that our writer says, "In the passion narrative, I experience again that feeling of helplessness." Encourage participants to probe their own reactions as six volunteers read this story, dividing it this way: Mark 15:1-5; verses 6-15; verses 16-20; verses 21-32; verses 33-41; verses 42-47. Discuss these questions:

1. What kinds of emotions did you experience in each of these scenes as you imagined Jesus before Pilate, saw Pilate hand Jesus over to be crucified, watched as soldiers mocked him, witnessed his crucifixion, came to the realization that he was actually dead, and watched from afar as Joseph of Arimathea buried Jesus?
2. What emotions do you experience when you consider that your own sins were in part responsible for Jesus' death?
3. Perhaps the story of Jesus' trial, crucifixion, and death raises sad, negative emotions within you. What emotions can you focus on when you recall that Jesus died so that you might be put right with God?

Close the Session

Trace the final steps of Jesus in song.

Distribute hymnals and sing verses 1, 2, and 3 of "Go to Dark Gethsemane" (number 290 in *The United Methodist Hymnal*). Encourage participants to trace Jesus' steps as he moves from Gethsemane to Pilate's interrogation to Calvary. This would be especially effective if someone in the group could sing a solo as others mediated on the words and, as able, slowly walked around the room.

Suggest that participants reflect silently on Jesus' final journey and give thanks for the offering of himself that he made for them.

Offer a prayer.

Lord, we cannot begin to fathom the wondrous love of Jesus that caused him to leave his place of glory with you to become incarnate and willingly die so that we might be restored to you. We give thanks for this unimaginable love. Amen.

---

1. From *The New Interpreter's Bible*, Volume VIII (Abingdon, 1995); page 718.

7. Room at the Table

BIBLE BACKGROUND

One way to celebrate the Easter story is to give thanks that there is room at God's table for everyone. Peter learned this lesson to his surprise when God showed him a vision and then sent him to the home of a Roman soldier. This centurion, along with his household, received both the Holy Spirit and water baptism. Paul learned that by God's grace there was room at the table even for him. He had severely persecuted the church until he met the risen Lord and became an ardent follower. In Mark's Gospel, a heavenly messenger revealed to three women who had been close to Jesus that he had been raised from the dead.

Acts 10:34-43

These verses are from the lengthy account encompassing Acts 10 of Peter's interaction with the Roman centurion, Cornelius, and his household. The paths of these two men would never have crossed were it not for visions given by God. Peter moved far out of his comfort zone during a vision of a sheet containing all kinds of animals—including ones considered by Mosaic law to be "unclean"—accompanied by the instructions, "Kill and eat!" (Acts 10:9-16). In response to a vision of his own, the God-fearer Cornelius directed several of his men to go to Joppa to bring Peter to Caesarea (Acts 10:3-8). Once in Cornelius's home, Peter experienced a conversion, recognizing that God does not show favoritism to anyone. People of any and all nations who worship God and do what is right are welcomed into God's kingdom (10:35) because Jesus is "Lord of *all*" (10:36, emphasis added). Although the revelation of God's impartiality had a profound effect on Peter, it was not an entirely new teaching. The Old Testament contains many stories of non-Israelites who found favor with God; two notable "outsiders" include Rahab (Joshua 2:1-14) and Ruth (Ruth 1:16). As if to affirm their full inclusion, both of these foreign women are mentioned in the genealogy of Jesus (Matthew 1:5)!

Today's verses summarize Peter's sermon to those gathered with Cornelius. Beginning in verse 37, Peter reviewed the story of Jesus, starting with his baptism by John. Anointed with the Holy Spirit, Jesus traveled throughout Judea "doing good and healing everyone oppressed by the devil" (10:38). Peter made clear that he was not sharing secondhand information; rather, he had witnessed all that had occurred both during Jesus' life (10:39) and even after he was raised (10:41). The heart of the gospel message is found in verses 39-41: Jesus was hanged on a tree but "God raised him up."

Peter ended his sermon by saying that he had been chosen by God before all of the events had unfolded to preach to people so that they might know that Jesus was "judge of the living and the dead" (10:42). Moreover, Jesus did not appear out of nowhere; ancient prophets had testified concerning him. Everyone who claims Jesus is forgiven of his or her sins (10:43).

1 Corinthians 15:1-11

In A.D. 54 or 55 Paul wrote a letter to the church in Corinth, a diverse congregation that he had founded about three years earlier. The date of composition is important, because this letter predates the earliest Gospel, Mark, which was likely written in the late A.D. 60's before the fall of Jerusalem in A.D. 70. Thus, the summary in 1 Corinthians 15 likely reflects the earliest tradition of the Resurrection story found in the Bible.[1]

Paul stressed that the good news he had preached to the Corinthian church was the same message that he had received (15:3). He was not preaching anything new, since it was the same gospel that other preachers proclaimed (15:11). Nor was it different, since it was the same message he preached that had prompted them to believe initially (15:1-2). According to very early church tradition, the crux of the gospel message was that "Christ died for our sins . . . he was buried, and he rose on the third day" (15:3-4). These three actions—he died, was buried, rose—were said to be "in line with the scriptures" (15:3, 4). Paul continued by writing that these actions were attested to by Peter (Cephas), the Twelve, more than five hundred witnesses, James, all the apostles, and Paul himself (15:5-8)—each of whom had personally encountered the risen Christ.

Through this foundational message, believers "are being saved" (15:2). This good news continues to transform the lives of all who believe.

Paul's personal story in verses 9-10 can become a model for all believers, for the Bible story is most alive when it intersects with people's own stories. With Paul, all believers can claim that they are what they are "by God's grace" (15:10). By God's grace, this persecutor who harassed the church was transformed. Likewise, Paul wanted the Corinthians to recognize that they did not earn God's favor but were "being saved" because Christ died on the cross and God raised him up.

Mark 16:1-8

Mark's Easter story begins on Sunday morning, "the first day of the week" (16:2), as three woman go to the tomb. Mary Magdalene, James's mother Mary, and Salome brought spices to anoint Jesus for burial. In the haste to bury him before the beginning of the Sabbath, they had not had time to care properly for his body. Walking along in the dim light of dawn, the women were concerned about how they would get into the tomb because they knew the round stone that rolled edgeways in a channel to cover the opening was too heavy for them to move. Judging by their conversation, they certainly were not expecting to find that anything miraculous had occurred. Mark's point in verse 4 about the stone being "very large" was likely intended to squelch the idea that the body had been stolen.

Seeing that the stone already had been moved, the women went right in and were startled to find a white-robed messenger. He allayed their fears and announced that Jesus was not there, because he had been raised from the dead. The messenger showed the women where Jesus' body had been placed (verses 5-7).

The messenger gave instructions: The women were to report to the disciples (especially Peter) the news that Jesus was going ahead of them to Galilee, which was the place where he had conducted most of his ministry. At the Last Supper, Jesus had told Peter that he would deny him three times, which Peter did (14:30, 66-72). In that conversation, Jesus said to Peter, "After I am raised up, I will go before you to Galilee" (14:28). Peter possibly could have comprehended the news the women were to bring, because Jesus had foretold what would happen. Yet the women "said nothing to anyone, because they were afraid" (16:8). Although most scholars agree that Mark ended his Gospel here, additions were made early on to tell "the rest of the story." The women must have overcome their fear, for the disciples, though disbelieving at first, saw the risen Jesus and went out to proclaim the good news (16:9-20).

SESSION PLAN

Open the Session

Enlist a volunteer to read the introduction to "Room at the Table" in the student book.

Distribute index cards or small slips of paper folded like a place card for a table at a church dinner. Have participants think of groups of people who are often excluded from the church and/or society. Examples may include children; people with mobility issues; people who cannot see or hear well; newcomers to the community; those who speak a different language; people of a different socio-economic status than most of the church; people who cannot read.

Have participants break up into teams of two or three, and assign to each pair or trio one of the groups that you have mentioned. (If your gathering is small, consider assigning two or three to each pair). Have them write the name of their assigned group on the index card, and ask them to think of three ways that the church could be more open and accessible to that group. Place the index cards together on a table that you have set up.

Offer a prayer.

Welcoming God, we thank you for inviting us to your table. As we celebrate Easter, help us to invite others to your banquet by sharing the good news of Jesus. Amen.

Engage the Scriptures

Listen to a sermon.

Enlist a volunteer to read from "Who Is at the Table?" starting with "God had to prepare . . ." and ending with "came without objection' (10:28-29)." Ask another volunteer to read Acts 10:34-43. Then discuss these questions:

1. What lesson did Peter have to learn before he could preach to Cornelius and his household?
2. What did you learn about God and Jesus as you listened to Peter?
3. What questions would you have wanted to ask Peter?
4. What response would you, as a Gentile, have made to Jesus after listening to Peter? Why?

Discover God's inclusive realm.

Come to the session prepared to tell the story of Peter and Cornelius found in Acts 10:1-33. Emphasize Peter's reluctance to relate to Gentiles, a reluctance that God had overcome by giving Peter a vision of a sheet filled with animals, both clean and unclean.

Choose a volunteer to read Acts 10:34-43. Discuss these questions:

1. What had Peter learned about who is acceptable to God?
2. What did he tell Cornelius and his household about Jesus?
3. What credentials did Peter offer to show the authenticity of his proclamation?
4. Had you been present, what might your response have been?

Finish the story by retelling the events of verses 44-48 to show that God does indeed include everyone.

Tell stories of faith.

Point out that in 1 Corinthians 15:1-11 Paul was teaching the members of the church in Corinth by telling the story of his own faith journey. Choose a volunteer to read that passage, and encourage participants to listen for details that link the story of God's action with Paul's own story. Ask these questions:

1. What does Paul say to the Corinthians about Christ?
2. What does Paul say about his own faith journey with Christ?
3. Recall that Paul had severely persecuted the church. How was Paul changed when Christ's story intersected with his life story?

Provide several minutes of quiet time for participants to discern the most important points of the Christian story in terms of their own lives. Form pairs or trios. Give each person ninety seconds to tell how God has acted in his or her life.

Suggest that participants go forth to testify to the effect that Jesus has had on their lives. Their witness needs to be inviting so that others may want to meet Jesus or get to know him better.

Give the gift of good news.

Select a volunteer to read 1 Corinthians 15:1-11.

Ask: What good news did you hear in this passage? (Use the Bible Background to show how Paul's message is foundational for believers.)

Discuss the questions at the end of "What Is Your Story?" Avoid mentioning specific names or situations that could violate privacy.

Challenge participants to take the good news that Paul proclaimed and pass this gift on to someone who does not yet know Jesus.

Overcome barriers to spreading the good news.

Choose a volunteer to read Mark 16:1-8, which is the original ending to Mark's Gospel. Note that according to verse 8, the main response of the women to the news that Jesus has been raised was "terror and dread."

Enlist a volunteer to explain the meaning of "terror" and "dread" by reading the beginning of "Why Are You Afraid?" through "sometimes, it's terrifying."

Recruit another volunteer to read from the same segment, beginning with "We fear speaking . . ." through "bodies in our churches!"

Put the following question to the group: When the terror and amazement of God's good news seizes your life, what are you going to do? Explain that one way to answer this question is to identify and overcome barriers—real or imagined—that inhibit us from spreading the good news.

Invite participants to name some of these barriers for them, either as individuals or as a group. List the responses on a large sheet of paper.

Invite participants to suggest ways to overcome these barriers. Encourage them to tell stories of ways that they have successfully shared God's good news with others.

Journal about a terrifying experience.

Select a volunteer to read Mark 16:1-8. Note that these verses are generally agreed to be Mark's ending to his Gospel. The rest of the chapter was added later. (Use the Bible Background if you want to add more information here.)

Point out that Mark's ending is different from other Gospels in that the women fled in terror rather than return to the disciples immediately to tell the good news. Explore how the women were feeling and why Mark concluded his Gospel the way he did by asking participants to review "Why Are You Afraid?"

Distribute paper and pencils. Invite participants to write journal entries as if they were Mary Magdalene, Mary, or Salome. Suggest that they keep these questions, which you will post on a large sheet of paper, in mind as they write:

1. What were you expecting to find on that Sabbath morning?
2. What did you think when you saw that the stone had been rolled away?
3. How did you react when you saw the messenger in a white robe?
4. What questions would you have wanted to ask the messenger?
5. What prompted you to obey the messenger and eventually return to the disciples to report what had happened?

Form small teams. Invite volunteers to read their journal entries to their team.

Close the Session

Praise and thank the foundation stone.

Read Psalm 118:1-2, 14-24. Invite participants to respond by giving thanks for Jesus, the once-rejected foundation stone, by each saying one way in which he has acted in their lives.

Offer a prayer.

Lord, we give thanks for the crucifixion, resurrection, and ascension of Jesus. Empower us to go forth as joyous Easter people to tell this amazing story so that all may know the wonder of your boundless love. Amen.

1. From *Preaching through the Christian Year, B,* edited by Fred B. Craddock, John H. Hayes, Carl R. Holladay, Gene M. Tucker; page 229.

CPSIA information can be obtained at www.ICGtesting.com
Printed in the USA
LVOW04s2234300115

425031LV00003B/4/P

9 781426 785856